ONLY IN KEY WEST

Cheers!,
Mandy Miles

A hilarious look at island life and everyday living

Mandy Miles

Another great read by Phantom Press, Key West, Fla.
Available at:
www.amazon.com
www.phantompress.com

Cover photo and some inside photos by:
Rob O'Neal • roboneal.com
Cover design, graphics and layout by:
Danette Baso SilversInvitesbyDanette.com

TABLE OF CONTENTS

ACKNOWLEDGEMENTS

I'd like to thank the Academy…oh wait, that's the imaginary Oscar acceptance speech I've practiced while grasping a hairbrush (or a bottle of ketchup).

This book is an actual accomplishment, mainly because I can finally cross it off every to-do list I've made over the past year. If not for a special group of people, it would still be on that list instead of in your hands as a reader, and I appreciate the opportunity to introduce you to the chaotic little place everyone calls Key West, but that only a handful call home.

My parents, Bob and Mary Ann Bolen, are at the top of every list in my life. They were my first editors and are my forever fans. I'm the luckiest girl in the world to have them and only wish there was a way to say thank you for, well, every single thing in my life. They're also responsible for giving me a terrific big brother, Kevin, who has been my pro bono marketing consultant and webmaster.

My husband, Capt. Stan Miles, made my dreams come true by sharing his last name with me in April 2010 and by loving me completely through countless late laptop nights and through stressful afternoons of trying to come up with a column topic.

My friend and photographer extraordinaire, Rob O'Neal, says in pictures what I could only hope to describe in words. His photos are stunning and his generosity in letting me use them for this book is unparalleled. Thanks, Rob O., for making me look good (and for guarding with your life some of the photos that could keep me from ever holding public office).

Author, artist, entrepreneur and all-around great guy David Sloan was the first person to suggest years ago that I turn the words I manage to string together for the newspaper every weekend into a book — then, with my forever "man of honor," Gregg McGrady, made sure it actually happened..

The Anne McKee Artists Fund in Key West made this disorganized writer feel like an actual artist by providing a grant that helped make this book possible.

The Key West Citizen newspaper gave me the chance to write my very first "Tan Lines" column way back in the summer of 2001, then they allowed me to publish the columns in books, which wouldn't be possible without The Citizen, Cooke Communications, Publisher Paul Clarin and Editor Tom Tuell. Also, thanks to the ever-patient nighttime editor Stacy Rodriguez who has waited longer than she should have to for me to turn in my columns every Saturday evening.

Finally, to you, my readers, who are beyond amazing in your loyalty, support and interest in the thoughts I put to paper. This book became a collaborative effort with readers enthusiastically suggesting their favorite columns for inclusion in this second volume, and posting their title suggestions on my Facebook page.

So kick back, relax and welcome to a real life in Key West….

5

LAUGH WITH ME — OR AT ME

SEAGULLS HIT THEIR MARK — LUCKY ME

I manage to humiliate myself fairly often, so I wasn't all that surprised when a seagull at the Jersey shore recently relieved himself on my forehead. These things happen, but they always seem to happen to me.

There was the past entanglement with a folding chair that collapsed around my leg while I held a can of blue paint, or tried to. That didn't end well at all.

I've also walked across a crowded Simonton Street with a skirt lodged in my underwear until my friend bellowed "Hey, Mandy, your skirt's stuck up your ass," from his second floor balcony. At least that one was easily corrected.

And then of course, my crowning achievement, or career low, depending on your perspective was the terrifying surprise appearance of a giant, shrieking peacock just inches from my face. That was a big one, humiliation-wise, as it led to me not only falling down, but also wetting my pants in my friend's backyard.

On the plus side, my foibles over the years, many of which have been shared with about 10,000 Sunday readers, have made me pretty much impervious to embarrassment, and I can laugh at myself just as easily as I laugh at others.

The latest in my series of missteps happened a few weeks ago on vacation.

I found myself standing on a crowded boardwalk in Ocean City, N.J, a beach chair in each hand, and a glob of bird poop smack on my forehead. If that wasn't bad enough, I was grimacing in disgust as my husband spit a stream of water in my face to rinse it off.

It was quite the spectacle.

See, Stan and I weren't in charge of carrying towels back to the house. Our marching orders for the one-block walk were to bring two chairs and the cooler. Someone else was in charge of the towels, which were still in use on the beach about a mile behind us on the other side of the hot sand we had just crossed without shoes. There was no going back for towels, even if I did have a glob of poo in the middle of my face.

Stan tried futilely to pour water from a plastic bottle onto my forehead, but we needed more pressure to rinse it off, hence the spitting in my face.

I can't imagine what the throngs of passersby thought as they headed, blissfully poop-free, toward their boardwalk lunches or miniature golf outings.

As soon as my mom turned around and sized up the situation, she reminded me cheerfully that, "It's a sign of good luck."

What's good luck? A seagull pooping on my face, or my husband spitting into it?

Yes, the lore of shore towns everywhere tries to convince people that the birds have actually bestowed good luck upon their noggin. Damn birds.

But have you ever noticed that the poop-free person is always the one yammering on about good omens? Seems to me the only good luck in the situation belongs to them – for not standing where I was.

Ah, but it all worked out. Stan's aim was true. The poop was sufficiently rinsed for the walk home and there was a hot shower just a block away.

Comparatively speaking, this barely registered on my scale of personal humiliations.

I chalked it up to "these things happen."

I just don't understand why they always happen to me.

HOT STUFF

Butter makes everything better. Everything edible, that is. I wouldn't recommend it as a glass cleaner or laundry detergent, but as a flavor enhancer for soups, breads, sauces, meats and vegetables, it's tops.

It proved itself once again Wednesday night, when by some bizarre and frightening twist of fate, I ended up on the hot side of the table at Benihana Japanese Steakhouse.

Big Brothers/Big Sisters, that great organization that pairs adults with kids who can benefit from attention and time, (the group we always say we should become more involved with), hosted its annual Celebrity Chef Cook-Off, a fundraiser in which community members don the puffy chef hats and slice and dice their way through five courses while their friends drink cocktails and laugh.

I'm still not sure how I ended up as a "Celebrity Chef," but if that wasn't bad enough, the guests at my table were none other than the owners of Camille's and Mangoes restaurants. They're certainly two of my favorite spots, and Amy, Giorgio, Denise and Michael are four of my favorite people, but only because I know my place — in the dining room, at a table, holding a menu and choosing a soup.

I don't belong in anyone's kitchen. I wouldn't even venture into mine if it weren't for the Diet Coke and an occasional English muffin.

I have been slowly facing my fear of hot skillets and sizzling oil, and that metal thing that looks like an oversized nail file they call a zester. (Apparently, it's sometimes OK to consume lemon, lime and orange peels. Who knew?)

The first step was replacing the battery in my smoke detector and finding a new storage space for the stuff I've always stored in the oven. I'm ready to start practicing my cooking skills, but had planned to start slow — sautéed chicken, maybe a nice salad with some homemade vinaigrette. Instead I found myself standing behind a sizzling steel table at Benihana while wielding a spatula, a large fork and a knife sharper than any I should be allowed to handle. Apparently my culinary career was to be a trial by fire sort of approach.

But I did learn several lessons…

- The table that just fried an egg in four seconds is hot. It's best not to lean on it with the heel of one's right hand.
- It's easier to cut the tails off shrimp when they're lined up neatly on

9

the table — before they're jumbled into a pile of butter and soy sauce.

- Some people don't like chicken fried rice in their red wine.
- The little grains of rice that just came off the table that can fry an egg in four seconds are equally hot, and should not come in contact with that really thin skin on the inside of your wrist.
- Butter makes everything better, especially if I'm cooking. There was no shortage of fat in the food I served Wednesday night but we were raising money for the kids, not the heart council.
- The table doesn't get any cooler midway through the meal, and will burn the heel of your hand as many times as you lean on it.
- Ray and Patrick, the professional Benihana masters who supervised everything at my table, are really good at what they do and really patient with those of us who have no business being on their side. They saved the rice and kept me from serving rare chicken.
- The combination of good friends, a watchful eye, a great cause — and a lot of butter — is the perfect recipe for a great night. (A little aloe and vodka later on also helped.)

DROP IT

I gave new meaning to the term "dropped call" the other day and began to see the merits of some states' laws that prohibit cell phones while driving.

I was chatting amiably with a friend about nothing of even moderate importance. In fact, I believe I was defending my stance on the importance of eating Upper Crust pizza in the restaurant so as not to risk the steam in the delivery box making the crust soggy. In the middle of my discourse, I dropped the phone into the netherworld between door frame, seat and floor. I had to shout to my friend that I had dropped him and to hold on and then began the delicate task of retrieving the phone without pushing it farther out of reach.

It didn't work. The phone dropped to the floor somewhere under my seat and I shouted to my friend that I'd call him back before pulling over, stopping the car and retrieving the phone. (Yes, officers, I did stop safely to get the phone rather than weaving all over the road.) Such is not always the case.

When will I learn that in order to pick up something I drop from my bicycle, I need to get off the bike, engage the kickstand and retrieve, say, my $1.50 admission to the beach at Fort Zachary Taylor. Otherwise, I end up straddling the bike, it tips over and I'm a tangled, sweaty mess in front of the admission gate with a line of people staring at my ineptness.

Why is it always the most breakable item that gets dropped on cement while a rubber ball falls onto plush carpeting? Take for example, my adventure in a hotel parking lot last month in West Palm Beach. I had two plastic bags in hand. One contained dirty laundry and a wet bathing suit, while the other held a bottle of vodka. Guess which one dropped in the blacktop parking lot and formed a puddle around my feet.

And let's not forget my birthday party a few years back when I dropped a bottle of red wine someone had just given me onto the new white concrete of a restaurant's patio. It looked like someone had been shot as the crimson liquid pooled and stained the pure white. I of course gathered my gifts and friends and made a hasty retreat.

How many items must I drop in the aisles of Fausto's before grabbing a handheld metal basket when I enter? This also would save my forearm from regularly going numb as a I cradle a pint of ice cream, a frozen pizza and a gallon of milk, all with a roll of paper towels tucked under my arm.

And how many times have you had to retrieve something you accidentally dropped into the garbage can? I've done it with envelopes I've written phone numbers on, important tax documents and leftovers that I didn't realize "someone" was saving for a midnight snack. Everything depends on what the item lands on, and what's been put on top since then.

While we're on the subject of my kitchen trashcan, let me take this moment to formally apologize to my downstairs neighbor, who has suffered through five years of mayonnaise jars dropped on the floor, beer bottles clinking into the bin from shoulder height and shampoo bottles hitting the bottom of the plastic shower floor. He's also been shocked by the occasional thunder that is me getting tangled up as I step out of a bathing suit. After a few awkward hops, I succumb to gravity and plaster probably falls from his ceiling. He also gets an earful of ice cubes that seem to leap from the tray to the floor and then skitter underneath the counter. They are immediately lost until physics takes over and the frozen solid becomes a freezing puddle on the kitchen floor.

For all of these missteps and thousands more, I say, as we always say quietly upstairs, "Sorry, Eddie."

Although I know I won't learn anything from asking these unanswerable questions, perhaps we all will walk away from this with a new level of awareness: It is better to eat Upper Crust pizza in the restaurant to preserve the delicate crisp.

GOING GREEN

By the time you, dear readers, are thumbing through this Sunday paper with your morning coffee, our apartment should be a whole new color. I say "should" because one never knows how these home improvement projects will go. The more likely scenario is that half the apartment is a different color and the two of us are in a frustrated heap on a plastic-shrouded couch wondering why we started this stupid project in the first place.

It all started with a plan. The plan was for me to get up early on Saturday and finish this column. Check. It's now 7:30 a.m. and here I sit, quietly typing and glancing frequently up at walls that will be "mesclun green" by tonight.

13

Before we go any further, let's just clarify: Mesclun is a mix of salad greens; mescaline is the hallucinogenic ingredient in peyote. And while peyote may be infinitely more fun than a salad, it probably wouldn't bode so well for our living room project.

Step two this morning is for me to awaken my other half and head out for the necessary supplies, including a gallon of mesclun green, a gallon of white for the trim and a gallon of a different white for the ceiling.

So far, so good.

From the paint store, we'll journey to Home Depot for an extra-large dropcloth, rollers, trays and other items. Then, let the transformation begin.

It should be interesting. I say this because I've watched my parents work through these projects for the past 40 years of their marriage. Of course, I've only been around for 33 of them, but in that time I've witnessed the painting of five houses in four states, and my parents are still happily married and madly in love. But it wasn't always pretty.

I can only hope for similar results with this, our first tag-team home improvement project, because when I do them myself, things go horribly wrong. You may recall the bathroom-painting incident a few years back.

I was left to my own devices here in Key West while Stan went deer hunting for four days. I was going to surprise him with a new blue bathroom, and told myself I had a steady hand and didn't need to tape the edges of the walls with that expensive blue tape people are always touting. Besides, I had watched my mother pristinely paint all of our houses without so much as a drop of color landing where it didn't belong.

My dad and I aren't as fortunate. For us, paint literally jumps out of the can and into our hair. We are covered in color before we even touch a brush to a wall. You may recall that the bathroom project, which was detailed in this column space, included a harrowing encounter with a folding chair that closed on my legs while I held a large container of blue paint. And you may recall that the blue paint ended up in a large puddle on my feet, between my toes and on the bathroom floor.

It was a nightmare, as was the bathroom when I finished in utter despair around 4 a.m. The walls were blue, all right. Unfortunately, so was the ceiling, the windows, the molding and even, for a little while, the sink and toilet.

My deer slayer, while sweetly supportive of my efforts ("condescending" is probably a more accurate term), immediately asked why I hadn't taped the edges.

Things will be different this weekend, I'm sure of it. First of all, this project has been a long time coming. I've lived in this house for nine years and am ready for a change. He's lived here for two years, and is tired of hearing me talk about wanting a change.

We chose the color months ago, a nice sage-like green with white trim for the living room, and the reverse for the bedroom. (No word yet on whether the bathroom will be revisited.)

Now it's time to execute. I have promised to embrace the tape concept. I also have promised to invest in as large a drop cloth as possible and to stay off folding chairs. What could possibly go wrong?

So as you all settle in for tonight's Super Bowl, take a look at whatever living room you're in, and be assured it's in better shape than ours. Enjoy sitting on a couch that doesn't crinkle under a plastic drop cloth and savor the chips, dip and other appetizers that aren't tinged with small drops of mesclun green.

And keep in mind that the wedding invitations have not yet been mailed.

I'll keep you posted.

INEXPLICABLE INSECURITIES

I don't understand why the car companies can't come to some agreement and put the gas tank on the same side of every automobile. My Cavalier's tank is on the passenger side, but it's on the driver's side of my husband's F150.

You'd think this little discrepancy would be relatively simple to remember, yet I find myself glancing at the little diagram on the fuel gauge EVERY TIME I pull into a gas station to avoid the minor embarrassment that comes with pulling in the wrong way.

Last week, that minor embarrassment turned into major gridlock when I started to turn around for a different approach before realizing I was about to block two other cars into their slots. Sorry about that, folks. I suppose that little picture of a gas pump on the dashboard is more effective when consulted before committing to a pump, but hey, at least it's there, and when used correctly can help facilitate a smooth fill-up.

Unfortunately, no drawing in the world can ensure a smooth encounter with, say, a ski lift.

The harrowing contraption is another unending source of stress for someone who only skis every six or seven years. While everyone else is enjoying the view from the chair lift or reviewing a trail map, I am already tensely poised, leaning forward with my ski tips close together and a pole in each hand. I spend the entire ride visualizing an uneventful dismount. As we approach the summit, I take a deep breath and try to stand up casually without crossing my ski tips or running over my own pole tip.

I often manage to pull it off; but there have been some admittedly unfortunate flailing incidents, only one of which required the operator to stop the lift while I extricated myself.

I've become accustomed to these little embarrassments and have learned to recognize the potential for awkward calamities. But the constant anticipation of them has given rise to an assortment of irrational little insecurities.

For example, I'm always afraid someone will think I'm stealing if I put my sunglasses into my purse while walking through Walgreen's or CVS. So I simply leave them parked on the top of my head, where they constantly slide off. I've never stolen anything in my life, and have never been accused of it, so who knows where this little paranoia started.

And am I the only one who waits for someone else to reach for their water glass at a banquet table? I never remember whether my glass is to the right or left of my plate, so I let someone else make the first move, and then I mentally calculate which glass goes with which seat and finally reach thirstily for mine. Of course, if the first person gets it wrong, we're all screwed, because someone on the other side of the table will know the proper etiquette and jam up the whole thing.

Granted, it would be easier to simply learn where the water glass goes, and remember it. But if that goes as well as the gas tank thing, there will be chaos at the next Chamber of Commerce luncheon.

And while we're on the subject of these irrational neuroses, does anyone else get just a little self-conscious when selecting songs on a jukebox, especially when no song is already playing? There's obviously not a bunch of previously chosen songs in the lineup, so the whole bar or restaurant soon will know which songs you picked, and there's a certain degree of responsibility that comes with those quarters. For example, no one is going to select an Air Supply song, even if they can sing along to every verse of "All Outta Love."

No, jukeboxes seem to be reserved for the universally "cool" songs by the likes of the Grateful Dead, Springsteen, an old Eagles song or some cherished summertime anthem.

I also get a little insecure when discussing movies with people who call them "films." Those conversations invariably start with the other person ticking off a list of movies, asking if I've seen them. After I've said "no" to the first three, and fully exasperated the condescending filmie, I just start lying and say yes to the fourth or fifth cinematic miracle. By then, they know I'm lying and I don't even care, so I quickly realize that I have to use the bathroom or refill my drink and beat a hasty retreat in search of someone whose movie enjoyment includes such classics as "Weekend at Bernie's" and "Ferris Bueller's Day Off."

Unfortunately, you can't lie your way out of the embarrassment that comes with falling asleep on an airplane so that your mouth hangs open, or your knee jerks violently into the seat in front of you.

That's just humiliating, and we always look around sheepishly to see who noticed the drool escaping from the corner of our mouth.

These are the irrational things that I think about, and they take up an inordinate amount of my time. And considering the number of times

I've run out of gas, perhaps I should spend more time looking at the actual gauge than the diagram of the tank.

In the meantime, I'm going to listen to Air Supply in the privacy of my own home, and watch movies that have no chance of ever being called films.

ADVENTURES IN POTLUCKS

They ate my flan. This was cause for an absurd mental celebration that can only occur at the end of a potluck gathering – but it doesn't always happen.

A recent Cinco de Mayo luncheon at The Citizen was one such gathering that of course touched off the usual internal conflict that settles within me as soon as the list of contributors and dishes starts circulating through the office email web.

We all know I'm no culinary genius, but what makes my nervous anticipation about my flan's popularity even more ridiculous is that I bought the damn dessert at Publix. I didn't make the yummy Latin dessert by hand. I separated no yolks, I measured no vanilla extract and I didn't have to distinguish between condensed and evaporated milk. So what the hell do I care whether people at my office chose to dip into the plastic container of golden, store made goodness?

I may be crazy for caring about a store bought offering, but I can't be the only person who delights, just a little, in providing a popular dish. You should get inside my head when people come back for seconds of something I actually cooked — in my own kitchen — using a real recipe. The little voice inside my head hisses, "Yessss!" and I secretly clench my fist in victory. Of course, if someone asks who made the delicacy and then compliments me personally, I offer my sincere thanks with a practiced nonchalance while trying desperately to restrain myself from enveloping the person in a smothering, swaying hug while tears of joy and relief run down my cheeks.

I try to act casually; as if people are regularly impressed by my cooking; the culinary equivalent of, "What, this old thing?"

These potluck successes – and the casual acknowledgement of compliments – come naturally to some people. They know their dish tastes good, and they know people will be talking about it, urging others to try it and going back for seconds. Still, I can't help but think they too rejoice just a little when retrieving the empty platter that was their potluck contribution.

If you think about it (and clearly I have), a potluck provides an accurate and honest assessment of a dish. No one is forced to be polite by eating whatever disaster is heaped on their plate. You can skip over some things by mumbling about a crowded plate and round two.

19

Once seated, you're free to ignore the little mound that turned out NOT to be tapioca pudding with shredded coconut, but rather some sort of dubious fish dip. And we all know what happens then: a new plate. We stuff the paper plate, upside down, into a nearby office trash can and start fresh for our next trip to the makeshift buffet table that doubles as a long cabinet in our office.

I have to say, our office puts together a fantastic potluck every few months, and there's usually no skipping or tossing. On May 5, I indulged in a scoop of Publix flan and noticed that others were also enjoying it. I know I didn't actually cook it myself, but at least I had chosen to buy something that was a hit.

I did celebrate my own, homemade success a few months ago during a Spam potluck party that required all guests to bring a dish made from the canned meat that gained popularity during World War II. Our friends Tom and Myrla hosted Spamapalooza in honor of the lean economic times, and I was a wreck the afternoon of the party.

First of all, I didn't grow up on Spam, which, by the way, gets its name from combining the words "spiced ham." My mom, thankfully, never served the fried slices of Spam, or the Spam sandwiches my friends remembered, so this strange meat in a pop-top can was all new to me.

I turned naturally to the Internet with its thousands of Spam recipes, and opted for one that called for diced Spam, Pillsbury Crescent Rolls, tomato sauce, cheese, pepperoni and mushrooms. Once I combined the ingredients and rolled the resulting paste into the doughy triangles, I was convinced the result would be inedible.

I quickly learned that the smell of Spam does not appeal to me, and I couldn't get past the sound it made slurping out of the can. Luckily, Stan is my guinea pig, and has bravely tasted everything I've cooked. His reports on the Spam Crescent Rolls were extremely favorable, so I felt OK about my Spamapalooza contribution. Amazingly, others agreed. I was beside myself when one party guest went back for a third Spam Crescent. Life was good.

And it's getting better. We're just about moved into a wonderful new, two-bedroom place on South Street with laundry facilities, a pool, dishwasher, central air and tons of other upgrades. I'll miss my Simonton neighbors, but will visit frequently.

I've also just finished setting up the new kitchen with our new dishes, silverware, pots and pans (weddings are great for that, by the way) and have promised Stan I'm going to improve my cooking skills while he fishes a marlin tournament in the Bahamas.

This is something I want to do for myself, not something he's requested. So if any of you, dear readers, have any recipe suggestions that would be good for a starter wife, please send them along. I'll be sure to report on my progress and the outcome — the good, the bad and the ugly. I'll try anything — chicken, fish, vegetables or appetizers — but I'm not much of a baker. That's just too specific for someone like me, so I'll leave the flan to Publix — and I'll leave the Spam in its can – on the grocery store shelf.

Bon appétit, Key West!

MOVING IN TOO MANY DIRECTIONS

You know how every house has a "junk drawer" for keys, wallets, scissors, rubber bands and loose batteries? I currently have four such junk drawers.

Such is the result of someone with a limited attention span trying to move into a new house all by herself.

While my new husband is off catching blue marlin and winning money in the Bahamas, I have been sweating my way from Simonton to South Street, heaving boxes, gathering fishing rods and tossing clothes in whatever drawer has room. I stopped counting at 37 trips up and down the steps on Simonton Street to the pickup truck waiting below.

The movers took the last six (and the heaviest) items to the new house. You may have seen them – they were the ones using a rope to lower an oversized blue couch over a second-floor balcony on Simonton Street when it wouldn't fit out the door without removing a bunch of molding. Of course, that removal was impossible because all the tools had already made it to the new house.

Then came the disaster that was me unpacking, trying to bring some sort of order to the chaos of furniture, boxes and bags. I had to trip over our tent three times before finally stowing it in a closet.

It's the attention span problem that gets me. That and the overwhelming hopelessness that descends on the resident of a new house when there is absolutely no sanctuary of solace and order. I had to focus. I knew that.

So I started in the bedroom, which was to be my retreat once the days of work and evenings of unpacking were over. I had the best of intentions in the bedroom, and started putting drawers back into the appropriate dressers.

But within 20 minutes I found myself sitting cross-legged in the living room thumbing through a high school yearbook. The book had never even been in the bedroom, which would partly have explained my detour.

Somehow, the "junk" that belongs in the coffee table cabinet had ended up in one of my dresser drawers. (I say "somehow" knowing full well I was the one who stashed the remotes, pens and notebooks in a fit of getting everything down to the truck.)

While traversing the 15 steps to the coffee table to install the junk in its

23

proper place, I slammed my toe into the shelves I had removed from the bookcase for easier transport. This mishap, of course, led to the familiar sputtering/hopping dance that takes place every time I stub my toes.

Once the dance ended I immediately placed the shelves in their rightful slots in the living room bookcase to avoid a repeat injury. (Notice I'm still in the living room and not the would-be bedroom sanctuary.)

Then, by some miracle of fate, a box of books had actually ended up right next to the bookshelf. Naturally, I began lining them up neatly in their proper place – until I came to the set of four hardcover yearbooks from Bishop Eustace Preparatory School.

It was all over. I sat cross-legged on the living room floor and went back in time to senior year. It was an exhausting trip, and one that made me realize how far I've come since that senior class trip to Disney World.

I'm now happy to report that much has been accomplished since last weekend, and a good deal of order has been restored to my life. The kitchen is put together, the living room is nearly complete and the bedroom just needs a few wall hangings.

There are still four junk drawers in the pantry, but things are working out perfectly, as long as no one enters the guest room.

I figure Stan deserves some of the adventure I've been experiencing in recent weeks. He's got quite the "honey-do" list to tackle upon his return. But at least we'll both be home, and as long as he's next to me, home is my favorite place in the world – no matter how many junk drawers we have.

WELCOME TO MY WORLD

ALL IN

Extended eye contact leads to a quickening pulse, and sly glances evolve into intense stares. There are periods of anticipatory silence and hesitation, punctuated by abrupt bouts of delight, relief — or disappointment.

It's not sex, it's poker and everybody's doing it.

The game can cost you, and copious amounts of alcohol doesn't make it any easier, only more reckless — and more fun. This island has learned a whole new vernacular in the past two years since Texas Hold 'Em has swept the nation. We're tossing around phrases like, "all in," "big blind," "chip bully," and one of our group's favorites after winning a big pot of chips: "Rake 'em on down here."

The games happen on different nights, at different times with different stakes. They're happening constantly on television and online. It happens for me every Friday, when about nine of us show up to pass money back and forth, insult each other and make the best hand possible out of the two cards in front of us and the five on the table.

This is, of course, easier if you're someone capable of remembering the markings on the two cards in your hand. I am not one of those people. Ask anyone. I'm a reasonably intelligent person who can manage to find my way through foreign airports, string some words together in coherent sentences and even pitch a tent. I can remember my kindergarten teacher's name, my parents' anniversary and the fact that adult male hippos eat 100 pounds of vegetation per day. But my mind goes blank just moments after I look at the jack of hearts and nine of diamonds that the dealer just placed on the green felt in front of me 14 seconds ago.

I'll look at those two cards repeatedly, but they never get any better. Of course, that doesn't mean I fold them like an intelligent card player. I'll stay in with a perplexed look on my face just to see what happens. It's usually nothing good. But every once in a while, playing poorly pays off and I win an unlikely hand, earning the privilege of saying, "Rake 'em on down here" as better players (i.e. everyone else at the table) shake their heads in disbelief and curse under their breath at my dumb luck.

Our game, like most others around town, has a set of house rules. We play over a tile floor, so glass is not allowed. Cocktails and wine are to be in plastic, and drinks are not to be passed over the table, which has remained in pristine condition, due in large part to the house rules. We don't use the cup holders provided around the table, but instead keep drinks on small tables scattered conveniently around the table. Wrestling is not allowed. Yes, it had to become an official rule for obvious reasons that involved a lot of cleaning up and a significant delay of game.

If you win the first game, you have to stay for the second unless you announce your intended departure before the first cards are dealt. Drinks are encouraged. We like to keep a relatively even playing field and sober people tend to pay more attention. But if your head hits the table and remains there for more than three seconds, you're "all in," meaning you have just bet all of your chips on the cards that are now stuck to your forehead.

Technical debates over split pots and misdeals are settled by an official copy of "Robert's Rules of Poker," but only after the dispute has lasted more than five minutes and the volume has increased considerably as everyone offers simultaneous opinions.

And finally, whoever goes out of the game early will, at some point, be making cocktails or shuffling. It's the right thing to do.

So shuffle up and deal.

FIGHT NIGHT

I admit, it's not something I ever thought I'd watch, much less enjoy. For a long time I referred to the phenomenon known as Mixed Martial Arts, or Ultimate Fighting, as archaic and barbaric, with a side order of homoerotic thrown in.

My guy friends would gather at someone's house for a Pay per View night of bloodletting, body slamming and bruises that swell the eyes shut. They drank beers, (my friends, not the fighters) they made lewd comments about the "Octagon girls" and any other girl on the screen and generally behaved as expected. I rolled my eyes and told them to call me when it was over, when everyone had finally "tapped out."

But I was hasty in my judgment and I admit it.

I've actually been watching a bit of the sport and have come to realize the degree of skill and athleticism involved. These guys, at least my two favorites, know wrestling, boxing, jujitsu, judo and have the mental ability to block out extreme pain and forget about the sweaty guy pounding their face into mush.

I'm not condoning this as a safe backyard competition and it should probably come with a disclaimer on the screen to prevent kids from practicing horrifying things like "arm bars," "body slams," and "rear naked chokes" (told you there was a homoerotic factor thrown in) on their friends and younger siblings.

There also are professional referees keeping a close eye on the fight. Their job is to determine whether a fighter is still able to defend himself – or remember his name – before stopping the fight. The referees take their job seriously, as the credibility of the sport ultimately depends on people not getting hurt or killed.

That said, I do have a few suggestions for the world of ultimate fighting. Consolidate. There are a million different leagues with slight rule variations. There's UFC, Pride, WEC and a bunch of others.

Now a few words for the fighters themselves. And for the record, no, I do not think I could do things better and I will not climb into the octagon to prove a point. I'm convinced girls are just a tad smarter than boys when it comes to these types of events. There are way better ways to spend a Friday night than being "mounted" and eventually beaten into "submission."

So to the fighters out there, some words of advice from a chick who would sit in the corner and cry as soon as someone wearing a mouth guard glared and shook their fist at her:

- Do not let anyone stand on your neck. Ever.
- Do not block punches with your face. It's a good rule in general, but it's also easier to breathe through your nose when it's not broken.
- Blood is apparently slippery, so try not to lose your footing on the mat when your own eye or nose is bleeding profusely and the other guy continues to pummel you. How rude.
- When seeing double, aim for the dude in the middle. (That one's from one of the Rocky movies, but it seems to fit here.)
- Arms only bend in one direction. When someone tries to change that, it's going to hurt. The same goes for the knees.
- There's no shame in tapping out, only in crying like a little girl and wetting your pants when you get kicked in the head.
- Kicking someone between the legs is a huge foul. But if you make it look accidental, the other guy gets a minute to recover. (Hardly seems long enough considering what a big deal guys generally make about that type of pain.) Nevertheless, use your opponent's pain – and rest time – wisely. And by wisely, I mean run. Consider how mad the other guy's going to be when the bell rings after you've just kicked him in an area meant to be treated nicely. There's no shame in running. Well, maybe there is a little.

As for me, I'll be watching from my couch and cheering on my favorites, Matt Hughes and Urijah Faber, silently urging them not to let anyone stand on their neck.

TECHNOLOGY HAS BECOME OUR ALIBI

I'll never know whether my friend's cell phone had truly been "screwing up" last week when he didn't return my multiple calls.

And I'll never know whether a genuine "Internet nightmare at the office" kept a local bigwig from responding to my e-mailed questions in time for a newspaper deadline, or if she was simply using technology to dodge the questions.

I call it electronic avoidance. We're not avoiding technology; we're using it to avoid people. Think about this for a moment: While modern technology has put us in touch with the world, it has also enabled us to avoid certain people in that world by providing caller ID and a litany of credible excuses.

Computers crash, servers go down, phone batteries die, calls are dropped.

How many times have you blamed Verizon, AT&T or MetroPCS, and feigned frustration with their spotty service that allegedly failed to register an incoming call or message, when in reality, the phones were working fine, but you had simply chosen to ignore someone's attempt at communication?

See? Electronic avoidance. We lie, we say we didn't get the message or see the missed call. We blame the phone company. We all do that, and so much more.

There's the blame-it-on-their-phone strategy that goes something like this:

You have dodged someone's phone call, so when you finally run into them, you play offense, not defense and immediately begin the conversation by telling them how frustrated you are with their phone and that you've been trying to reach them for days.

"What's up with your phone? I've been trying to reach you but I keep getting a weird busy signal."

There's also the voicemail excuse that goes, "Hey, I'm glad I ran into you because your phone won't let me leave a message."

This one assumes that you are on a voice-message basis with this particular person, because as we all know, in many circles, a "missed call" alert has pretty much replaced the message. I don't have to wait for my friend's outgoing message to tell me to leave a message, and I don't need to hear the electronic voice telling me which number I've reached. All I have to do is hang up and wait for them to scroll through their missed calls to see that I tried to reach them.

Of course, a follow-up text message may follow the missed call if a particular piece of information needs to be conveyed.

And while we're on the subject of texting, when did the world collectively decide to shun the letter "o" when replying "OK" to a text? Does it really take so long to type one letter?

I know, I know, some people with older phones are still forced to scroll through the three letters that correspond to the numbers on a dial pad, and one letter can actually require three presses of a button.

Text messages themselves are a form of avoidance, because they are a substitute for a real conversation. Admit it; we've all ignored a phone call and then sent a quick text to explain why we didn't answer. I didn't say the explanation is always the truth, but it apparently makes us feel a little less guilty for ignoring someone.

I must say, until recently I found myself usually believing someone else's technology excuse when they hadn't answered my call or called me back right away. I would even commiserate sometimes and compare communication difficulties.

In reality, I have no reason to believe these people's excuses because in some cases they're the same people I avoid and later lie to about why I haven't called them back.

Just as I glance at an incoming number and say, "Hmm, that's so-and-so. I'll call them back in a bit," so do they.

None of us will ever really know whose computer really died, who actually left their phone on a boat or whose phone service provider was having genuine trouble with their cell towers.

We'll never know, and it's probably better this way. We can all keep avoiding calls while protecting people's feelings.

Technology has made the world a smaller place, but that doesn't mean we want to speak with everyone in it.

GAME ON

Every once in a while it's nice to realize that we're not entirely grown up. The return of board games as an evening activity among friends is cheaper than a night on the town, but also a nostalgic reminder that some things never change.

For example, someone was absolutely convinced the other night that he had earned significantly more Trivial Pursuit wedges than were in his pie piece. We actually had to pick up the game board and move the couch to be sure the boy genius had not lost a wedge.

He hadn't. He also hadn't answered many questions correctly, but there was no need to point that out last week and cause further delays to the game.

It's not just Trivial Pursuit that still reduces us to bickering 11-year-olds.

The people with the most money and property in Monopoly are still unbearable (a little like certain "Boardwalk/Park Place" neighborhoods in Key West.)

The players who own the coveted blue properties, along with the greens and the yellows around the corner are still hiding money under the board and negotiating shady deals while they're in the kitchen making a drink. Then they change the rules to allow themselves to build two red hotels on one property, thereby doubling the highest rent that threatens to bankrupt the player (usually me) left with three railroads, the Water Works and Baltic Avenue.

Despite our age and alleged maturity, the game often ends in frustration and someone storming off.

Ah, some things never change. For instance, some Pictionary sketches are just as juvenile and anatomically ludicrous as they were in sixth grade. But now it's red wine that is accidentally spilled on the couch rather than Hawaiian Punch, and it's one of our best friends, not our parents, who gives us the warning look when we venture near the couch with a red drink.

Poker now costs real money, not buttons, and we actually play by the rules instead of guessing which hand beats which and changing that hierarchy every few minutes.

We couldn't have a discussion about games without mentioning the hold that Texas Hold 'Em now has on this country. It's no longer just a boys'-night-out game. Finally, lying really can be the best, and most profitable, option. But these poker games are intense. We are older, our voices are louder, our drinks are stronger and our bedtime is much, much later.

I, for one, am thrilled with the resurgence of game night. A few drinks, some mixed nuts and a little friendly competition is all it takes to bring friends together again in someone's living room.

Sometimes it doesn't have to happen at night or in a living room. We play Travel Scrabble on the beach regularly, and relish the jealous looks everyone gives as they walk past and comment on what a great idea it was to bring everyone's favorite word game to Fort Taylor.

My good friend, David, took us on a nostalgic trip through the intricacies of Freeze Tag last weekend in Orlando. The conversation stopped just short of all of us running through our friends' backyard, tagging each other and then crawling between their legs to "unfreeze them." We also rehashed the thrill of "Red Rover," which was a great game that never really got the credit it deserved. A few broken wrists should not have dampened its popularity.

And then there is the game that should be forever banned — Marco Polo. I never liked it as a kid, and am even less of a fan as an adult. It's bad enough when you're "It" in tag, but now you have to close your eyes and SWIM around trying to tag people. And let's not forget the repetitive calls of "Marco," and the relentless answer of "Polo" that echoes across the water for what seems like weeks at a time. That game must end.

But Trivial Pursuit will live forever...or at least until someone finally lands in the middle by exact count.

BUTTONS WE PUSH

While pressing the appropriate phone buttons the other day to check my alarmingly low checking account balance, I started thinking about how many buttons we push every day.

Our lives are controlled by buttons – at the ATM, the gas station, telephones, computers, iPods, radio stations and alarm clocks.

Every day begins with the snooze button for me and continues with the coffee pot, microwave and hair dryer (although I suppose that's more of a switch than a button).

Then it's out to the car, where I push a button to unlock the door, and another to change the radio station. By then, I've usually dialed my phone, retrieved a message or sent a text – all using buttons.

The office is a veritable hot bed of buttons, with a keypad security entry, computers, faxes and vending machines.

But none of it is exciting anymore. My brother and I used to fight over who would push an elevator button in a hotel, or who would enter the letter and numbers for the tabletop jukebox in a New Jersey diner.

We didn't care which songs our parents had selected, we just wanted to push the buttons.

34

Remember how exciting it was to get your first car with power windows and locks?

My blind, great-uncle owned his own stretch limo and driver. Well, of course he didn't own the driver, but he paid him well to drive him everywhere.

Uncle John would let the kids pile into the champagne-colored stretch and press every button we could find for lights, moon roofs, stereos, intercoms and the privacy window. It didn't matter whether the limo ever left the driveway.

My grandfather was a banker his whole life, and his garage and basement constantly were filled with intriguing adding machines, calculators and cash registers that made a satisfying click when you pressed the buttons. Some would even thrill us by printing out register tape. The grandkids would pull them all out, along with his pencil sharpener and blank ledger books for a big time of "playing bank" in Pop's den.

Another group of cousins got in trouble in Annapolis 25 years ago when we stayed at the historic Maryland Inn for our aunt's college graduation. The Maryland Inn was right downtown with a front porch lounge that our parents enjoyed for hours over cocktails and snacks.

The kids would pass by the table to grab a fry and a sip of Coke before heading back inside to the marble lobby – and to the ancient elevators with giant brass buttons.

We rode those side-by-side elevators up and down from the first to the sixth floor, stopping at each one in between.

There were multiple "Going down, thir?" Droopy Dog impressions, but it all ended when the hotel management reprimanded us and sent us out to the porch with our parents, aunts and uncles.

I hope kids these days appreciate all the buttons they have access to. And while most will never know the thrill of a tabletop jukebox, maybe they still enjoy selecting an elevator floor.

I know I still do. It's much less worrisome than checking my bank balance.

MY BUCK STOPS HERE

We're officially huge fans of the new Dollar Tree next to Albertsons, and judging from those of you I've seen in there, we're not alone in our budgetary enjoyment.

I can't believe it took so long to get one of these stores in our tiny, yet pricey, island village.

We've taken to stopping at the dollar store before Albertsons to see what we can cross off the list for cheap, and have had great success.

There have also been some dismal failures, resulting in a list of items that have proven themselves to be worth more than a buck.

I've mentioned in a previous column our mistake in buying generic cotton swabs rather than Q-tips. Anything else is just a stick in the ear. And now that we've finally made it through the box of cheap sticks with almost no cotton, we'll return to the brand name that's a part of every medicine cabinet.

There also was a shampoo/conditioner disaster at the Dollar Tree that ended up costing more in the long run. A cheap conditioner added knots rather than remove them, so I pitched the bottle when it was only half full and returned to a familiar and trusted name brand.

The $1 kitchen garbage bags leave much to be desired, as the drawstring closure pulls away from the top of the bag as soon as you deposit anything other than tissues.

Oh, and Fruit Rings are not the same as Fruit Loops. I repeat, Fruit Rings are not Fruit Loops, so don't be fooled by the similar red box.

On the other hand, Raisin Bran, Frosted Flakes and Alpha Bits from the dollar store taste just as good as the $5 boxes from the grocery stores. But we've found the best cereal deal in town at Fausto's, of all places. They have a giant box of IGA brand Corn Flakes for $1.89. Add a smattering of dollar-store honey and you're in business for breakfast or a midnight snack.

The generic, $1 toaster pastries certainly give Pop Tarts a run for their money. The cheap strawberry jelly works just fine, especially on a $1 loaf of wheat bread. I admit, I'm a bit of a peanut butter snob when it comes to Jif, so I've not yet tried the cheap version.

The Dollar Tree makes you realize how big the retail mark-up really is. We've gotten multi-vitamins, aspirin, dishwasher detergent, chips, cookies and condiments for a dollar each.

You can't beat the bargains, especially for little toys, craft items, gift wrapping and even flip flops.

I did do a bit of a double take when I saw a home pregnancy test for sale by the register. Those, like condoms, are things I'd be willing to spend a few bucks on.

And I'd love to hear a consumer report on the $1 batteries.

But I'd say we've saved at least $30 per shopping trip by stopping into the Dollar Tree and forgoing our usual name brands. It's definitely worth it, and I say, "Welcome to Key West."

Just stay away from the Fruit Rings. Trust me on this.

GOD, GRANT ME THE SERENITY...

OK, we've got a problem of epidemic proportions that could bring this tightly packed little island to its knees. We've been ignoring it for awhile now and side-stepping the issue for our own convenience rather than taking the time to address it for the greater good.

I know you can't help someone until they're ready to help themselves and admitting you have a problem is the first step toward solving it, so maybe I can help move the process along a bit

I admit it: Thousands of you have a problem.

It overwhelms and paralyzes you with anxiety and prevents you from achieving your goals and reaching the destinations you seek. It affects your family, friends, neighbors, even strangers passing on the street.

You and countless others suffer from this malady that could cripple an entire community:

You suck at parallel parking. There I said it.

I don't mean your tire occasionally rubs the curb, or that you sometimes end up a little cock-eyed but still well within the confines of the parking space.

Those little miscalculations are to be expected when people are accustomed to pulling into spacious driveways and garages and they're easily forgiven.

I'm talking to the folks who have no clue how to even begin the task, and even less understanding of the subsequent steps necessary to insert their vehicle smoothly alongside the curb and between two other cars.

Has the world simply given up?

I keep hearing people talk about the fancy new cars that parallel park themselves on dense city streets, and that's all well and good – for the people who own those cars.

But here's a news flash: Your 2001 Ford Focus didn't come with that option. You should be able to wriggle that little car into a downtown spot all by yourself. And just so you know, some people actually manage this with just one try.

Yep, they identify a spot that will accommodate their vehicle. They pull alongside the car parked in front of their chosen spot. They turn around, grip the passenger headrest with their right hand and place the left hand at the top of the steering wheel.

They then back halfway into the spot while turning the wheel to the right.

Now pay attention, this is important: They straighten out the wheel before the tires hit the curb and the car ends up sticking out at a 45-degree angle with nowhere to go but the sidewalk.

If you stop "cutting the wheel" in the middle of the spot, and not when you hit the curb, then you'll still have room behind you to straighten the wheel – and the car.

Obviously, these things take practice and some people have a more natural feel for it than others. I grew up in a town that required tight parallel parking skills every summer, so I got a lot of practice. I also heard the things people sitting on front porches say while making fun of the parking-challenged.

I actually park much better than I drive – ask Stan. He's regularly impressed with the spots I've squeezed into on the first approach. (He's less impressed with some of the situations I've gotten us into while driving at a high rate of speed.)

For those who struggle with this seemingly monumental task; you know who you are. Actually, the whole town knows who you are. You do realize we can see you when you back directly into the curb three times before giving up and skulking farther down the street in search of an actual parking lot. Also, just so you know, some people don't like it when you use the back or front bumper of their car as a guide while you bump your way back and forth into the spot.

Now that we've identified the problem, let's work on a solution and start practicing parallel parking for one hour a day – somewhere other than in Old Town.

Eaton Street nearly ground to a halt last week while one whole lane waited for a woman (I hate to admit it was a female driver) to make six attempts on a spot 50 percent longer than her car. Of course, we couldn't go around her a.) Because there was oncoming traffic, but b.) Because we never knew when she was going to accelerate erratically out of the spot and begin a fresh approach.

She was visibly distressed, which of course didn't help her decision-making or execution of the task. After her fifth try, I actually stepped out of my car and offered to park the car for her. She refused, apparently unaware of the gridlock forming behind her.

The woman finally gave up and pulled away in a huff. Apparently, she'll have to hit rock bottom before she'll change her ways. She also refused to admit she was powerless over her problem and did not accept help from a higher power (in this case, me).

But it's not too late for the rest of you. Practice. Get help. There's no shame in asking.

But there's plenty of shame in backing directly and repeatedly into a curb while traffic piles up behind you and people mock you from their front porch.

KEY WEST: SUNDAYS IN PARADISE

PARTY'S OVER; PLEASE PUT YOUR CLOTHES BACK ON

It's all over; you can open your eyes again.

Anyone reading these words on Sunday in Key West has apparently survived another Fantasy Fest.

Surviving is one thing, but I wouldn't call the weekend a rousing success if you're only reading this because you didn't know what day it was until the newspaper thwacked you in the face as you slumped in someone's bushes early this morning.

Oh well, at least you're still in one piece, even if your disassembled costume is strewn piecemeal around the island and some of your body paint remains on that menacing curb that appeared out of nowhere and tripped you around 3 a.m.

As soon as you can pry the tongue from the roof of your mouth and loll your head to the side, you can evaluate the situation and assess any damage. If you made it home or back to a hotel room (preferably your own) with your wallet, camera and phone, then congratulations; you're in better shape than about half of your costumed cohorts right now.

Those unfortunate souls will spend much of today in anxious misery, retracing their sodden steps in a hungover effort to reclaim any number of lost items. Of course, having seen many of this year's aquatic frolickers, I think it's safe to say that even the most exhaustive search will never return the dignity that many of you left in the curbside muck to be discarded unceremoniously by this morning's valiant clean-up crew.

Having just survived my own 13th Fantasy Fest, I still have to wonder at the decisions some people make during this last week of October in Key West:

• What makes anyone think 65-year-old breasts that hang to the waist will look better if painted to look like tulips and then put on swinging display at lunchtime on Friday? And they seemed genuinely surprised when no crowds of camera-toting men stopped them for photos and leering comments. Go figure.

• What makes people decide that their 6-pound wiener dog will enjoy navigating a sea of flip flops and dodging stilettos while being blasted by hot air bellowing from the food booths of the street fair? Come on, folks. That crowd is no place for a tiny dog. The hot dog will be flat as a patty melt.

• What mother decides that Duval Street on the Saturday afternoon of

Fantasy Fest would be an appropriate place for a stroll with her 5-year-old daughter?

• Why do some people insist on making their lives difficult with a costume that requires about 37 props, a long tail and a mask that eliminates peripheral vision? Think about this, people. This may be your first Fantasy Fest, but it's not your first Halloween or costume event. Comfort is key. Besides, no one wants to hug you by the end of the night, as sweat pours from your wig and your detached tail is tucked under your arm.

• Why don't more people stay until Monday and thus avoid what must be an absolutely miserable Sunday morning departure? I realize it's not always an option, but more of you really should consider it for next year. I can't imagine doing what I did last night and then hearing the insistent knock of a hotel housekeeper around 9 a.m.

But hey, at least once your bags are packed and your room is vacated, you get to drive 40 mph for several hours as an unending line of traffic snakes its way slowly along the island chain. So you've got that going for you.

You guys have my deepest sympathy, but I'm really glad I'm not you this morning. I may have made some questionable decisions myself this weekend, but I made it home with my wardrobe – and dignity – intact, and from the comfort of my couch can now savor a decision I made 13 years ago – to move to an island that truly welcomes anyone.

Thanks for coming to our party, everyone. We hope you had a great time. Now put your shirt on and be on your way – you're in our parking space.

Last word…

This column appeared the Sunday following Fantasy Fest 2011, which was anecdotally described as one of the more unattractive gatherings in recent memory. People were walking around naked during the Goombay festival the weekend before the official Fantasy Fest parade. While I applaud the courage and self-confidence of these people, I won't pretend to understand it. Is there such as thing as too much self-esteem?

roboneal.com

ATTA BOY

Did you happen to notice the revolving spotlights circling the downtown sky Thursday night?

I was drawn to them as if they heralded something important; something out of the ordinary.

They did not disappoint.

Key West does some things really well. We're not so good at coming to a decision about how much tourism is enough, and we really can't figure out what to do about the homeless population. But we can sure as hell throw a party and toot our own horn.

There was a lot of both going on Thursday night at the San Carlos Institute as the makers of the documentary "Key West: City of Colors" gave the town its first glimpse of the hour-long film at a premier gala complete with red carpet interviews, glittering sequins, daring outfits and eye-catching jewelry. The film uses the unfurling of the 1.25-mile-long rainbow flag down Duval Street as the backdrop for a character study of an entire town that came together one day in June 2003 to make its own rainbow.

The island's true colors shone brilliantly in the film, leaving the eclectic and enthusiastic audience on a high that would last far after the credits rolled to the top of the screen.

Drag queens greeted moviegoers. Men in leather chaps leaned down to delicately kiss the cheek of the town's 92-year-old mayor emeritus. An 82-year-old woman who has spent her whole life in Bahama Village carefully navigated the stairs of the San Carlos, helped by a lesbian in a boa and everyone else who passed near her. Politicians, writers, photographers and people from Ohio who were just curious to see what was going on all converged in an anticipatory crowd and spoke of the "big to-do."

Key West, the entire town, became a movie star Thursday night.

"It really made me proud to live in Key West," was a comment heard over and over as people rehashed their favorite parts and congratulated friends who were featured in sincere interviews in the film.

We wandered through the crowd in the 500 block of Duval Street, sure of ourselves and reminded in no uncertain terms that we made the right choice in deciding to live in this ridiculously expensive, frustratingly chaotic place. And even the next morning, when the spotlights were

45

turned off, the red carpet was rolled up and Duval Street was once again itself, it still looked damn good.

Perhaps we shouldn't need an entire documentary or a gigantic rainbow flag — the largest in the world — to remind us how much we like this place. But this is Key West, and we've never been known for subtlety.

And in true Key West style, who did the flag organizers find to sponsor the unfurling event for a whole bunch of money? Absolut Vodka, of course. God bless those folks from Sweden who have been catching our eye with their magazine advertisements for years.

An entire film highlighted the town's history, people, influences and multiple personalities. But that film may never have been made, and there would have been no reason for the Thursday evening celebration had it not been for one man's idea more than three years ago.

Nothing would have happened and no memories of color spanning 14 blocks would be etched in our minds if Gregg McGrady hadn't sat down one day and wondered aloud, "Wouldn't it be cool to have a rainbow flag stretching the length of Duval Street?"

The idea nagged at him for awhile as he did some research. His sewing skills nearly nonexistent, Gregg realized the project would be a huge undertaking — and it was. But it happened. Hundreds, if not thousands, made his idea happen during the town's Pridefest celebration on June 15, 2003 and everyone who wandered down to Duval Street that day will never forget the colorful sight.

I know I never will. And I want to take this time, space and opportunity to thank my friend for making that memory possible with a single idea. Talk about pride.

Atta boy, Gregory. I love you.

roboneal.com

AH, AUGUST

The saturated air feels too thick to breathe. Afternoon storms wring out the clouds in sudden but selective downpours that drench only one neighborhood at a time, and those damn, teeny-tiny ants show up en masse for their annual and relentless summertime infiltration.

You know the ones I mean. These blasted things are so small it takes a second glance to be sure you've even seen something move. Then upon closer inspection, you notice a few more, moving jerkily, but in the same direction, following some invisible route down a wall to a seemingly insignificant crack or barely visible seam.

The visible ones are easily wiped away with a squirt of 409 and the swipe of a paper towel, but their previously unseen comrades return within minutes, traversing the same microscopic super-highways along the tile behind the sink or down the side of the cabinet behind the trashcan.

And what about the one that manages to climb onto your hand to save himself from the 409 swipe? You feel, or at least think you feel, a tiny tickle, like a stray hair. You're still looking for the errant hair, grabbing lightly at your forearm with your fingertips, when you feel it again – you think. Finally, you spot the little bugger and wipe him away like a grain of sand.

These ants are a popular topic of conversation among Key Westers in August. I'll always remember a hilarious column by former Paradise columnist Leland Hurd, who shared the various home remedies she had heard suggested over the years for their removal.

I, too, had been in the throes of an invasion, so I laughed with relief and empathy at Hurd's description of one particular eradication attempt. It involved filling the ants' secret crevices; the ones at the end of their busy thoroughfares; with ground cayenne pepper.

To do so, the amateur exterminators were instructed to blow the spicy powder into the holes using small straws. Hurd hysterically described the scene that was unfolding in her Key West apartment just as a visitor; her mother perhaps, arrived, and thus encountered the writer and her friends darting into the corners of the kitchen with small, powder-filled straws pressed to their faces.

Given the Conch Republic's historic and much-publicized involvement with a specific type of powder and its associated small straws, the visitor was understandably concerned about Hurd's lifestyle choices here at the end of the road.

Oh I laughed. And I still mention that column, written probably a decade ago, when the conversation invariably turns to these uninvited summertime guests. I've even researched them and written a news article about the miniature, but ultimately harmless invaders.

I've heard them called sugar ants, crazy ants, ghost ants, you name it. Then again, newspaper policy prohibits me from printing some of the names my husband was using for them the other night around 11 p.m. when he launched an all-out defensive assault, vowing to drive them from the premises if it took all night, and it nearly did.

Stan, with reading glasses on and a magnifying glass in hand, was scrutinizing every corner of the kitchen and shaking his head in wonder and frustration at the puny army marching in long, single lines to various base camps.

The obvious and initial 409 swipe is always my solution – out of sight, out of mind; at least for an hour or so. But Stan foraged under the kitchen sink and emerged triumphantly with a tiny container of the serum – Terro.

Those of you in the know are now nodding sagely, having found the elusive solution. Everyone else, listen up. It's a clearish gel substance that must be like heroin to a tiny ant. They can't get enough of the stuff when a few drops are placed on small squares of cardboard placed strategically in their popular kitchen hangouts. They then take the stuff into their secret crevices and get their friends hooked until they all overdose.

After more than three hours of Terro placement, strategic adjustments in their locations and close monitoring, Stan was sufficiently satisfied with the ants' consumption to come to bed.

He repeated the assault the next night with some modifications and on the third night declared a tentative victory over the undersized enemy. I swear I saw a tiny white flag waving from the seam between the counter and sink. But then I felt a hair tickling my wrist.

Ah, summer.

First of all...

OK, so I cheated. This column wasn't technically a "Tan Lines," as it ran on the front page of The Citizen in March 2007 – the day after Kenny Chesney gave an unforgettable, free concert at Jimmy Buffett's Margaritaville on Duval Street.

Citizen photographer Rob O'Neal secured us front-row positions two feet from Kenny, and once in place, we didn't dare relinquish our spots. This, of course, led to a certain limitation in our alcohol consumption, as neither one of us was prepared to fight the crowds and make our way through the second-floor maze that leads to Margaritaville's bathrooms.

I never thought I'd say this in reference to a nearly alcohol-free concert, but it didn't matter one bit. Thanks, Kenny.

COUNTRY MUSIC STAR GETS UP CLOSE AND PERSONAL

It took a few seconds to figure out why no sound was coming out of my mouth Sunday morning. It's Kenny Chesney's fault.

The country music star took the stage at Margaritaville a little after 9 p.m. Saturday and didn't stop playing his own country hits and other summertime anthems that took me back to college until midnight.

I can't imagine how it feels to hear so many people singing songs you wrote, but it's got to be all right for the guy from Luttrell, Tenn. He wore flip flops, drank beer and told jokes. He grabbed women's cell phones and said hello to crazed fans from all over the country. He laughed at inside jokes with his band members and only left the stage once — to go to the bathroom.

On Saturday night, Chesney wasn't the untouchable country music Entertainer of the Year. (Well, he still is that.) But he wasn't untouchable. He wasn't playing to a sold-out football stadium, and the stage he and his guys crammed onto had to be smaller than any they had ever shared. He was just a great guy playing songs everybody loved.

I could not have been closer to the singer without security getting

involved, and I was having a blast. The sweating, swaying, singing crowd was having a blast. And most of all, the guys on stage were having a blast, or at least faked it pretty well. They strayed from the set list, laughed when they played the wrong verse and called for another bucket of beers.

These are guys I'd hang out with; guys doing what they love, and it was a treat to see. It was however, slightly disturbing to see some of the most crazed fans I've ever seen at a concert. It reminded me of Beatles footage of security guards pulling swooning women out of the crowds. It must be a little unnerving to have women wiping the sweat from your face and saving the towel. Other women looked like they were near tears as the smiling, blue-eyed singer slowed down for an acoustic set while his band took a well-deserved break. It was a little creepy to be honest.

Sure, I'd love to hang on a boat and have a few beers with the guys (assuming someone would pull out a guitar at some point.) But let's not get crazy. The night was a perfect combination of music. From favorite country hits that threatened to get me thrown out of my native New Jersey, to the edgy Violent Femmes' "Blister in the Sun," I never stopped singing.

Actually, I did stop to stare in open-mouthed amazement during guitarist Clayton Mitchell's "Crossroads," but then lost my breath when Chesney and his right-hand man, Tambo, launched flawlessly into U2's "With or Without You." There was Steve Miller, Bob Marley and every other song of summers past.

There was also a tribute to our host for the evening, Jimmy Buffett, although Chesney was taking his life in his hands when he chose, "Why Don't We Get Drunk," as there were plenty of willing fans to fulfill the song's suggestion.

I was just glad to be there.

AIRPORT ARRIVALS NOT THE MOST HOSPITABLE

Has anyone been to the airport recently to collect a visiting relative or returning roommate? What a horrible experience.

Don't get me wrong. I'm a huge fan of the new Conch Flyer bar and restaurant in the new departure terminal with its comfortable gate area.

Unfortunately, almost every time a local departs Key West, they also have to return to Key West, and therein lies the problem. A friend last week literally had to jump into my moving car, a duffel bag in his lap, while a sheriff's deputy in a car just three feet away bellowed, "Make it quick, make it quick," through a loudspeaker. Really? A loudspeaker?

Can someone please explain how we're supposed to pick up someone when we're not allowed to stop, even for 10 seconds, anywhere near the airport doors? I didn't even have to open the trunk, load any luggage or get out of the car to hug someone, and I was apparently taking way too long.

I shudder to think of the cop's reaction if I was welcoming two friends with two small kids, a stroller and a thousand other requisite items. I'm pretty sure his head would have exploded. And I must have missed the public meeting when officials apparently decided that taxis can park alongside the curb for half an hour awaiting the arrivals, but regular folks have to circle the property 11 times before driving past and waving to their emerging out-of-town relatives because the officer on duty won't let anyone stop – ever.

I don't get it. If there is some traffic plan for arriving passengers, please let me know. Let's hear it – and let's install some signs to explain how the hell people are supposed to get into their friends' cars.

Because, honestly, the deputy I encountered last week offered no explanation or guidance, but rather a short-tempered command to my frazzled friend to, "Make it quick."

Oh, and I got an aggressively amplified "Move out now," during one of my loops around the terminal. I had made the egregious error of stopping for pedestrians in the crosswalk, and when I didn't plow them over at the sight of blue disco lights in my rearview mirror, the officer took to barking into his loudspeaker.

Like I said, if there is a traffic plan in place, let me know. I'll even help spread the word in this column space.

I'm just relieved I was picking up a returning local and not a first-time visitor. I would have been truly embarrassed by the treatment we received.

Of course, I have nothing against the cab drivers. They earn their living at that airport and deserve a designated waiting area.

And I understand there are strict security requirements in place at all airports.

I can even sympathize – to a point – with the rude cop, because I know that many people's IQs simply plummet when they travel.

But the Key West airport is, for many weary, rum-seeking travelers, their first glimpse of our island home.

So let's not force them to leap into a moving vehicle. Not yet, at least. Let's see how they act downtown.

And another thing...

This column garnered perhaps the largest response of any of the 300 or so that I've written. I was certainly not alone in my experience and frustration, and received 23 e-mails from people agreeing with me. I forwarded the responses to airport officials (to prove I was not alone in my rant) and am happy to report that the situation improved dramatically within two weeks. Turn the page for the full results.

EFFECTIVELY DEMANDY

Well done, everyone.

Good things started happening at the airport once I casually mentioned there was room for attitude and parking improvements. The squeaky wheel gets the grease, and I can damn sure squeak. Just ask my parents, my husband and the former boyfriend who called me "Demandy."

But this was a team effort on the part of me and so many of my readers, so I'm happy to share the good news I received on Friday: New parking spots will be established for people picking up arriving passengers, new signs are being installed and we can expect a kinder, gentler police force directing traffic.

Wow, Christmas came early in Key West.

For those of you just joining this discussion, let me explain.

A few weeks ago, I wrote a column about my horrible experience at the airport while picking up a friend who was returning home from vacation. There was no curb space to pull over and allow my friend to get into the car. So when I saw him walk out the front doors, I merely paused in the next traffic lane so he could climb in. He had no luggage, so there was no trunk-popping and loading. He was a returning local, so there were no hugs or extended greetings. He just had to get into the car.

Oh, and it was 10 p.m. on a Wednesday – not exactly what I would call "peak hours." In fact, there was not another car in sight behind us – except the cop and his blue disco lights. There was a trio of people traversing the crosswalk in front of my car and heading toward the rental cars. While stopped for these pedestrians, my friend hopped into the car and had his door closed well before the last pedestrian was safely across.

Nevertheless, any casual observer, upon seeing the vein pop out on the deputy's forehead, would have thought I had abandoned my car in the middle of Times Square on New Year's Eve after plowing down 30 people.

He yelled, waved his arms and bellowed; "Move on," through his in-car loudspeaker. He couldn't even see that there were pedestrians in front of me, but his blue lights certainly illuminated my scofflaw friend, who had the audacity to get into the car once I stopped for those in the crosswalk.

It was ridiculous. I was embarrassed at the greeting our visitors receive at the airport if they have the gall to accept a ride from their host friend, rather than shell out 15 bucks for a cab.

So I squeaked. And by that I mean I wrote. I detailed my experience, voiced my frustration and asked the powers that be to design a plan for passenger pick-up. I also promised to help spread the word in this column space and tell the locals about whatever plan materialized.

But I did not squeak alone, and our combined voices turned into a roar.

To date, I have received more than 18 emails from readers who had received the exact same treatment at the airport. My Inbox that Sunday afternoon was filled with messages titled "Thank you," "You tell 'em," and "Airport issues."

I enjoyed the support I was getting from readers, and County Commissioner Heather Carruthers was working on getting to the bottom of things, but I hadn't heard a peep from airport officials or the sheriff's office – until this past week.

Airport Director Peter Horton mentioned my less-than-complimentary rant during a recent Chamber of Commerce luncheon, apparently thinking I was the only one who was unhappy. Afterward, I took the liberty of forwarding him all the messages I had received from similarly frustrated readers.

One woman wrote that her elderly mother starts worrying about the Key West pickup process when she boards her plane in Michigan. Another reader – and writer –compared the law enforcement officers to the Gestapo, while another resident was tired of being treated like the enemy, especially from people whose salaries we pay.

Mr. Horton, now convinced that I was not the only one complaining for lack of a better column topic that week, forwarded the emails from my readers to Lieutenant Mitch Snider, head of airport security for the Monroe County Sheriff's Office.

And things started happening.

"He says his headquarters higher-ups have been all over him to improve officer demeanor here at the airport," Horton wrote to me about Lt. Snider. "We had a meeting with him this morning, and he laid out the changes (no whistles, no waving of the arms, no shouting at drivers and passengers, etc.)."

Lieutenant Snider wrote to me on Saturday, and promised that he's doing his best to balance safety issues with other considerations and their impact on the public. He has directed his officers to remain curbside and spend more time enforcing the new rules regarding cabs and vans and less time enforcing minor traffic violations.

Snider also told his people that they are to offer helpful instructions about where to park, rather than pointing out the traffic violation of stopping in a roadway or crosswalk.

Thank you, Lieutenant. Thank you. And, yes, I look forward to sitting down with you soon to review additional positive changes at the airport. I can also assure you I am not the only one who appreciates your attention to this matter.

Mr. Horton's message to me continued to detail other significant improvements being made at the airport for the benefit of local drivers.

"When we complete these changes, there will be six curb spaces for immediate passenger pick-up, eight spaces in the rental car lot along the front row, for a half-hour of free parking for those who need more time to load up and of course dozens of one-hour-free spaces in the west lot (40 yards from the arrival door.)"

In addition to the new parking options, crews are installing large signs this week letting people know about them.

"We hope these two initiatives on the part of both the sheriff's office and the airport will solve the problems that we've been having with passenger pick-up congestion...," Horton continued.

Thank you, Peter. Thank you. I believe those initiatives will work, and I appreciate you guys making things better out there.

In the meantime, let me know if you need further assistance spreading the word. I can squeak mighty loud. Thanks again for your attention to this matter.

Signed,

Demandy

roboneal.com

FIRST TIME

When was the last time someone told you how lucky you were to live here?

I love those conversations, when a sunburned visitor who's genuinely enjoying himself marvels at those of us who left friends, family and the expected life behind to head south. The same people drive rental cars on Flagler Avenue and view Key West High School as a curiosity.

"They have school here? How cool would it be to say you went to Key West High School?"

They compare it to graduating from University of Tahiti (which actually doesn't sound too bad, either.)

I recently participated in one of these conversations with a kindly man who was staying for two weeks. He was shrugging out of a jacket at the airport and hailing a taxi, torn between diving into his hotel pool and heading to the Hog's Breath on a friend's recommendation. He had never been to Key West and hadn't even made it out of the airport, but was telling me how lucky I am to live here.

I was actually jealous; jealous of his fresh perspective, his wide eyes and his unblinking acceptance of all things warm and sunny.

We sometimes lose the delight we once had, but a recent birthday gathering of good friends turned nostalgic, and we started thinking back.

Remember the first time you got a local's discount without having to tell the waitress you lived here? And then remember the first time that waitress had your Diet Coke, lemonade or iced tea waiting on the lunch table before you picked up the menu you had memorized?

Remember the first time you read all the wall memorabilia at the Green Parrot? And then, remember the first time you walked in and knew more than half the people there? And for the guys out there, remember the first time you noticed the "Providioms" poster above the urinal in the bathroom? (I've only heard tell of its existence).

Remember the first time you met Captain Tony?

I was walking in front of Bayview Park with Citizen photographer and columnist Rob O'Neal. I was new in town and we were covering the Labor Day picnic when Rob saw the legend approaching and asked if I wanted to be introduced.

"Are you kidding? You know him?" I said, impressed with my friend's connections.

One kiss and several invitations to Vegas later, Tony and I were fast friends, and I'll treasure him always.

Remember the first Thanksgiving you spent here on the island? Friends gathered around an outdoor table, showing up at different times throughout the day, bearing wine, fresh fish, pumpkin pie or sweet potatoes.

Remember the first time you received a warning instead of a speeding ticket because you knew the police officer, or the first time you knew the author of a Letter to the Editor?

Remember the first time you saw your best friend wearing a tie and didn't know whether he was going to court or a funeral?

Remember the first dolphin you saw from the deck of a boat, or the first manatee that sighed from under a pier.

How about the first time you saw a shark at Rock Key, a turtle at Joe's Tug or a Navy SEAL parachuting into Fort Taylor?

I know there are more Key West "firsts" yet to come, and there always will be.

So the next time we run into someone new, let's not tell them how great this place used to be. Let's let them know how great it still is...and then send them to the Green Parrot bathroom.

TIME MARCHES ON

Eleven years.

That's almost as long as it takes to get through this country's public school system.

An accountant named Norm Peterson spent 11 years on the corner stool in a Boston bar where everybody knew his name. And for 11 years, I've had a Florida license plate on the back of my car.

This week marks the 11th anniversary of my move to Key West in July 1998. And while I won't bore anyone, myself included, with clichés about how quickly time passes, the impending calendar date recently gave me pause.

A lot can happen in 11 years. In that time, I've had two cars. A red '94 Saturn took me from Jersey to college in North Carolina and then as far south as the road goes. A '98 Cavalier is still getting me around despite a few troublesome noises and a window that doesn't always go up.

Cars don't generally get better with age, but other things do, like friends. I've lived among a core group of 11 (there's that number again) irreplaceable people in Key West almost since the day I arrived. They've been partners in crime, shoulders to cry on and faces that have provided a million smiles and corresponding memories.

Together, we've seen it all. Years and memories are piling up on each other like shoe boxes filled with pictures, and I recently started thinking about the numbers of the life they represent.

In the past 11 years, I've lived in three apartments with four different roommates. I've had two bikes, including the current blue Simple 7-speed that was stolen just a few months after one of those 11 friends gave it to me for my birthday. It was found with the help of this town and the guys at The Bike Shop, but only after a generous stranger offered to buy me a new one simply because he wanted to help.

Admittedly, this place can be frustrating as hell, but it still pretty much rocks. I've had only two full-time jobs during my southernmost residency. True, I've been a writer at The Citizen since I unpacked the Saturn on Ashby Street, but I left the news world for two months in the fall of 1999 to work at the Mel Fisher Maritime Museum. I quickly missed the day-to-day insistency of news and returned to The Citizen, grateful for the new friends I had met at the museum.

I've participated in 11 Fantasy Fests. My parents happened to be in town for my first, which was their last. All I knew then was that the town had "some big block party around Halloween," so I thought the timing of my parents' visit would be perfect – not so much. I should have done some research. My parents now visit every February, which is good because hardly anyone gets naked for Presidents Day.

I've dealt with two major hurricanes and a few minor ones, and I hope to never again see the looks of utter despair that creased people's faces in the wake of Hurricane Wilma's floodwaters in October 2005. Their homes and cars were under water. Their keepsake memories were warped beyond recognition or washed away entirely. But we survived and we got through it together.

I've had four serious boyfriends and attended nine weddings. The fourth boyfriend turned out to be the last, and soon will become my first — and only — husband.

I've written one book, thousands of newspaper articles and 132 checks to Keys Energy Services. Actually, the first 36 or so of those were made out to City Electric, remember them? I've interviewed four seated mayors, four police chiefs and three school superintendents.

I've used seven hotel pools as an unregistered guest, and gotten one speeding ticket. I've bought more than 40 pairs of flip-flops, but I still use the same blue canvas beach chair that my brother gave me when I moved here. It, too, seems to get better with age, and over the past 11years that chair has become my own corner bar stool — in a town where everybody knows your name.

Thanks, Key West, for the past 11 years — and counting.

ONLY IN KEY WEST

Sometimes you just have to shake your head and smile in this town.

I just got back from a week at the Jersey Shore, where I happened to pick up a copy of the local newspaper and saw an article about the Ocean City Town Council.

I must say, there was nothing exciting on the agenda, and I dreaded the thought of having to actually cover that meeting and write something about it for the next day's newspaper, as I do every other Tuesday for the Key West City Commission meetings.

That's not such a problem here on this little speck of limestone that dangles like an afterthought from the southern tip of Florida. We're not usually lacking for "colorful" issues to debate, legislate or prohibit, and that makes my job as a city government reporter a lot more interesting.

For instance, I'm willing to bet none of our Key West city commissioners expected to hear testimony from a man painted silver and wearing a purple leisure suit in Old City Hall last month. Nevertheless, they each listened earnestly as Robert Matheson, the Silver Man, shared his opinions about proposed new rules that require a certain amount of distance between the Silver Man and say, the Dirty Joke Guy, when both are performing on Duval Street.

Only in Key West.

And I guarantee you the Ocean City Town Council never had to hire a chicken catcher or develop a chicken relocation program. But our commissioners muddled through it, while a city official found a farm in Eustis, Fla. that wanted our noisy birds. (No one mentioned the fact that the farm sounded a lot like the one that welcomed every little kid's aging dog at one time or another. But I hear some chicken enthusiasts actually visited the place and saw many of our local feathered friends alive and well.)

Only in Key West.

The city commissioners also acted, years ago, to protect the city's palm trees from the homeless people who kept ripping them apart to weave the hats and baskets they sell on Duval Street. Now the palm weavers are included in the new street performer ordinance, and there are laws that govern the length of palm fronds that can be harvested.

Only in Key West.

Every town has some type of special-event permit required for parades, boat shows, block parties and craft fairs.

But what other locales issue permits for races featuring drag queens in high heels, bartenders chugging beers for charity and a dachshund parade?

Only in Key West.

Where else do city officials use the word "nipple" and "genitalia" during an official, public meeting? Our leaders recently held an hour-long discussion to define nudity, and decide how to regulate it during Fantasy Fest.

They also touched on the two required public hearings necessary to finalize legislation about dogs in bars. (They ultimately voted unanimously to let dogs be nude in bars – OK, I'm kidding about that one.)

Only in Key West.

Has any other county library had to pass a rule that requires visitors to actually read, not sleep, while soaking up the county's air-conditioning so as to prevent homeless people from nodding off behind their newspapers?

And where else have the panhandlers gotten in trouble at the city's southernmost point for offering to take pictures of tourists, and then extorting money from them? There's now a law prohibiting that.

Only in Key West.

Yes, we are truly unique, and one need only attend a City Commission meeting to be reminded of it.

Then again, a simple stroll down Duval Street would provide the same reminder in less than a minute.

We've got a staggering assortment of people, some just a little crazier than others, but things move along rather nicely for the most part, with far less friction than you'd expect.

Some things could only happen in Key West. We're one of a kind, and we wouldn't want it any other way in any other place. Everyone somehow fits together on this tiny island – even if the Dirty Joke Guy has to stay 10 feet away from the Silver Man.

CLOSE TO HOME

Stuff like this doesn't happen in our country. Mother Nature likes us better. Our buildings are stronger. Our warning technology is more sophisticated. Our hospitals are more advanced and our supplies are unending.

But the people we're seeing on television right now are speaking English, wearing Nikes and carrying all their belongings in Gap bags.

These people are Americans and but for a slight change in the wind direction, that town could be Key West. We could be hungry and displaced, searching for relatives dead or dying. So let's cool it around here and relax for a second.

You in the blue Honda, there was no reason to give that guy in the Hummer the finger on Thursday. Yes, he pulled into the panic-stricken gas line in front of you and, yes his car holds considerably more gas than yours. But things could be worse.

We're OK.

You in the big Dodge Ram, did you feel like more of a man as you plowed through that flooded intersection following the afternoon downpour? Did you enjoy sending whitecaps over and under the little green Nissan that almost stalled? Ease up, guy. Wipe that smirk off your face, and remember that such areas are No Wake Zones after a thunderstorm.

There's been a lot of those flooded intersections lately with heavy rains landing on an already saturated ground. But things could be worse.

We're OK.

Yes, we're dipping into retirement funds to fill up our gas tanks in preparation for a possible hurricane. But there are no fuel leaks throughout the city. It's hot and steamy and our tempers are short. We're sick of the summertime weather and the sauna that hovers after the rain. But we're not hacking through our attics to escape rising flood waters. (There IS a guy screaming from his upstairs balcony on Simonton Street, but he does that all the time.)

Our mayor has not ordered everyone to abandon our beloved waterfront city in the wake of shooting, looting and desperation borne of true disaster. Our relatives are not missing or decaying in flood waters. Our hospital remains open and well-equipped. Our police officers can still help. Some of our roofs have leaked. Carpets got damp and cars stalled. There were more leaves in the yard than usual and the pool guy may have shown up late. Our mocha chip ice cream melted in a power outage last week and intermittent darkness was inconvenient.

But we're OK.

On a brighter note, beer was only $4.74 for an 18-pack of Bud Light bottles last week. There was a rainbow over the lollipop-colored houseboats at Garrison Bight and the Cancer Foundation won $15,000 in a charity poker tournament when a Key West resident decided to give something back to the community that helped him two years ago. So for the next few weeks (or months), let's relax. Don't be so quick on the horn or with the finger. Help someone — with anything — here or somewhere else. Walk or ride a bike when you can. It might take a little longer or be a little hotter, but things could be worse.

We could be on the other side of the Gulf waving for a helicopter or drinking contaminated water like the refugees we usually only read about on other continents. But catastrophe has ravaged our own country this time.

Stuff like this does happen here, and not everyone is OK.

GIVE ME A SIGNAL

Did I miss the memo or accidentally delete the e-mail announcing the island's abandonment of the turn signal?

I don't get it. Granted, this town has never been a bastion of conscientious driving, but we at least had managed to jiggle that little stick by our left hand to alert fellow motorists to an upcoming change in direction.

Not anymore. I've come to view the blinker as the exception rather than the rule in recent months, and it seems more locals than visitors are skipping this important step. It's done with a sort of arrogance, as if to say, "I live here, I know where I'm going and I don't have to tell you."

Locals have stopped using blinkers, while tourists on rented scooters and electric cars never turn them off, so anyone following them down Simonton Street expects them to turn right onto Eaton, no, Fleming (I hope not; it's one-way), maybe Southard, nope, wrong again.

Let's find a happy medium.

This blinker observation led me to consider other traffic annoyances on this little speck of limestone.

For instance, let's talk about scooters taking up a full-sized parking space in a shopping center. This has to stop. I guarantee anyone who drives a scooter, rented or otherwise, listed parking as one of the reasons to justify the vehicle, so start using the smaller spaces reserved for it. It's so disappointing to approach a seemingly empty parking spot and pull halfway in, only to nearly collide with a blasted scooter, sitting primly in its roomy spot.

Then we have to back out, straighten out the car and figure out what to do next – but only after we've rationally ruled out the option of continuing forward and simply pushing the tiny thing out of the way.

Speaking of pushing things out of the way, that's apparently what some people plan to do any time they attempt a left turn onto North Roosevelt Boulevard when exiting the Albertsons parking lot near Radio Shack. This should be outlawed. And any driver who lets someone turn left in front of them should be shot. That driveway should be used for right turn exits only. Any questions?

And while we're on the subject of North Roosevelt Boulevard, let's remember, folks, that the middle turning lane is your friend when you're turning left onto the boulevard from, say, McDonald's. There is no need to wait for a break in both directions of traffic. Treat the situation like a game of Frogger, and first aim for the safety of the middle lane, and then navigate the next row. There's no sense holding up the entire line of cars behind you while you wait for traffic to ease up in both directions.

Another group that should be aware of the line of cars piling up behind them is the pedi-cab drivers. Can you guys move over just a tad when there's a break in the parked cars alongside you? Seriously, you've got 16 cars behind your left shoulder waiting to pass while you cruise in first gear down Duval or Simonton. We're waiting patiently to pass your damn wide rickshaw without slamming head-on into an approaching vehicle. Can you just give us a little space when you're passing a loading zone, empty parking spot or other curbside gap? Is that too much to ask?

Would it also be asking too much to request that all non-police, government vehicles be painted something other than white? Do we have to make them all look like cop cars so they all can bring about that moment of panic when we see them in the rearview mirror? No, I'm not implying that I speed or regularly break other traffic laws, but come on, we all tense up and slow down at the sight of a large white sedan in our rearview, and what harm would be done by blue aqueduct authority cars, yellow Keys Energy vehicles and brown or green city Public Works cars? Just a thought.

Despite all this, I wanted to end this week with a positive thought on our island driving characteristics. I have to say I'm always quietly proud of the drivers in this town every time I see a whole line of us stopping to let a chicken cross the road with four or five downy, little nuggets in tow.

Who doesn't sit back for a minute, rest their hands on the steering wheel and just sort of smile at the little feathered family? It always brightens our day for a little while – at least until the guy in front of us decides to yank on the wheel and execute an unannounced left turn.

roboneal.com

GREAT MINDS THINK ALIKE

I recently overheard a great bartender telling a customer that he had a master's degree in history. He winced guiltily, acknowledging that his parents may not have gotten their money's worth from the investment they hoped would lead to a law degree. But the engaging thirtysomething guy then spent the evening smiling, laughing and representing all that is right with Key West.

His story is not unique. Hundreds of people in this town have college transcripts and parchment degrees that to an outsider make them ridiculously overqualified for their current job – or jobs. Accounting majors drive parasail boats while people once bound for law school happily mix drinks or distribute pool towels at local resorts. Political science majors and Shakespeare scholars drive taxis, sail schooners or sing the songs of summer at local watering holes. I love that, and it works. Why? Because they're all smiling.

The vast majority of these so-called overqualified workers are genuinely happy to be an integral part of this fierce little speck of limestone that thrives at the blue-green intersection of the Atlantic Ocean and Gulf of Mexico.

"Life's too short to shiver," one of my best friends says each night when customers in his taxi ask what brought him to Key West. (Granted, his unmistakable Boston accent makes it sound more like, "Life's too shawt to shivah," but we get the point.)

There's an equalizing force at work in Key West that supersedes the loftiest of degrees from the most elite universities. We came because we wanted to, not because we were expected to. And we stayed, not out of habit, but out of the sense of belonging we felt soon after we made our first friends.

Just because many Key West residents have the education and credentials to climb corporate ladders or litigate other people's lives doesn't mean they have a desire to.

And the most important lessons can't be taught in a college classroom. Look what we've all learned from this island and from each other.

We've all developed a more accurate gay-dar than anyone in any suburb, and we've learned that two moms or two dads are just as good at raising kids as heterosexual couples. We've learned to question our elected officials, and we do so every other Tuesday night at City Commission meetings. We've also learned the consequences of NOT questioning them.

We've learned we can't pump untreated sewage into the ocean if we expect to be able to swim at our beaches. We've learned how to get rid of mold in the aftermath of a flood and we've learned how good our neighbors really are. We've learned what happens when an inflated real estate bubble suddenly pops, and we've learned to park in the shade in the summer months.

These and so many other valuable lessons come from lives being lived on this limestone, and I value the education that continues every day.

I also know I've never seen a lawyer with a smile as contagious as the one the bartender wore last week while mixing drinks after spending the day on the water with friends. Life was good for him. So were tips, by the way.

His parents may not have gotten the expected return on their investment, but if all they wanted was for their son to be truly happy, then they're now worth a fortune, because our smiles are priceless.

FAMILY: IT'S ALL RELATIVE

roboneal.com

Mandy and Mom, 1977

BECOMING MY MOTHER AN HONOR

Women often joke about doing their best to avoid becoming their mother. They say they won't use the same "Because-I-said-so" rationale with their own children, and they'll remain more current and "hip" to the world of teenagers.

I don't have any kids yet, but already I'm seeing my mother in myself.

I made her trademark chocolate birthday cake with butter cream frosting last week, but realized my icing-writing skills need some work.

I make the same spaghetti with meat sauce, although hers still tastes better when consumed in our familiar kitchen at the Jersey Shore. No, it's not some secret family recipe for homemade sauce that takes all day on the stove. It's a can of Ragu, traditional flavor. But we brown our own meat, thank you.

We express frustration with our other halves with the same sharp intake of breath that lifts our shoulders and is followed by a frustrated sigh.

71

We both ride around with near-empty gas tanks to the unending exasperation of those same men.

We both love the "Wizard of Oz" but cry when Dorothy says goodbye to the scarecrow.

We fold towels the same way (in thirds) and share an aversion to ironing, although she stoically spent four years pressing the white Oxford shirts I wore with my high school uniform once it was no longer cool to be seen in the "wash-and-wear."

She made sure my field hockey, basketball and softball uniforms were always clean for the next game and she and my dad had me at the gym by 6 a.m. some November mornings in the beginning of basketball season. One or both of them was always in the bleachers on game day.

She sat through countless airings of "Annie" when we got our first Betamax.

She taught me to read. She sat for hours on a porch trying to figure out how she, a right-handed person, could teach me, a leftie, to tie my shoes. (She apparently figured it out, and passed it on to me, because I'm not wearing Velcro sneakers.)

She caught me sneaking out of the house — or in.

She did it all, but still did more.

She moved halfway across the country to the vast Midwest, where she raised two kids with a traveling husband and her own mother thousands of miles away.

She put up with a dog she hated. (Wait, no one could hate Sneakers, but the two merely tolerated each other for 13 years.)

She later moved the kids, husband and dog back across the country, and into her mother's house at the Jersey Shore; the house that represented beach days, boardwalk rides and penny candy during our annual summer vacation. But this move was not a vacation; it was simply what had to be done in response to my grandmother's late-stage breast cancer diagnosis. My mom nursed her mom through the wrenching torture of chemotherapy and the eventual devastation that was breast cancer in the 1980s.

She managed to be a caregiver, a daughter and a mom all at once, and it wasn't until years later that I realized how permanently terrified she must have been. Death is brutal. It's rotten, and it smells; and my mom worried endlessly about how it all would affect her kids while at the same time losing her own mother.

72

And yet, when I think back on the 18 or so months we had with Grandma Bergren, it's not the pill bottles, the wigs or the aftermath of the chemotherapy appointments that I recall most vividly. Instead, I remember watching "General Hospital" with my grandmother after school while we both ate bowls of bananas, milk and sugar. I remember her spirited political debates with my dad and the realization that she and my mom have the same laugh.

"You do what has to be done, and then you move on," my mom says off-handedly when people remark on her quiet, inner strength and her fierce devotion to family.

She's taught more than 700 elementary school kids over the past 23 years while still managing to teach her own to do the right thing. (All right, so we don't always do the right thing, but we always know what it is, so she's done a damn fine job.)

She and my dad gave up their downstairs bedroom when my dad's mom could no longer live alone. My mom gave up her weekends, her vacations and her dinners out to ensure her mother-in-law's safety and comfort 12 years after doing the same for her own mother.

While others dread turning into their mother, I can only hope, and I know I'll be able to do whatever has to be done. I've watched a woman do it all.

Happy Mother's Day, to mine and all the mothers who give the best of themselves. I love you, Mom.

FATHER KNOWS BEST

When did our parents become so smart?

Mark Twain penned a theory about the intelligence of our fathers. He wrote that when he was 14, his father was so ignorant; he could hardly stand to be around him. But by the time Twain was 21, he was astonished at how smart his father had become, and how much he apparently had learned in seven years.

I've reached the point in my life when all the things my parents told me are proving correct, despite my best efforts to prove them wrong.

So on Father's Day this year, I've compiled just a sampling of some of my dad's wisdom, and favorite sayings. Some he came up with on his own, and some he has borrowed from others. Most of it generally drove me crazy as a kid, but like Twain, I am now astounded by how smart my parents have become.

Here's a sampling of the world according to Bob, which no doubt will make my mom cringe, as she has been hearing it all for more than 40 years.

74

"Never quit one job until you have the next one lined up." Sure, we've all imagined the perfect, dramatic exit that would have the most devastating impact on a soon-to-be-former employer. But the thrill of that departure won't pay the rent.

Rain won't make a clean car dirty, or a dirty car clean. Yes it may rinse the top layer of dust off my car in this drought, but that doesn't qualify as clean in my dad's book.

Just because the state of New Jersey had decided I could drive well enough to have a license, didn't mean I had passed my dad's test until I could change a tire, check my oil and navigate the 9th Street traffic circle in Somers Point, N.J.

"Stay to the outside, OUTSIDE, of a traffic circle." Dad imparted this knowledge when teaching Kevin and me to drive. The lesson included Dad stiff-arming the dashboard while screaming at us and stomping his foot uselessly through the floor looking for the non-existent brake pedal on the passenger side.

Never trust another driver's blinker.

"If you're going to wallow with the pigs, you have to soar with the eagles." This was his version of the hangover mantra, "If you're gonna be dumb, you gotta be tough," and was usually accompanied by him vacuuming our bedrooms at 8 a.m. and then suggesting a breakfast of buttered bacon and anything else that would turn our stomachs.

"There's not enough o's in the word smooth," he would say whenever pulling off some suave gift or surprise for my mom.

"Stan, you've got the football," he said as he walked me down my wedding aisle and handed me off to Stan as if he passing off the silver suitcase that holds the nation's nuclear codes.

Location, location, location are the three most important things in real estate. No, he certainly didn't coin this term, but he did make sure we knew it before we were 12 years old.

"Buy the best; only cry once," when it comes to spending more than my mom had approved on a new television or lawn mower that was supposed to last forever.

In sales, always give the customers a little more than they expect.

Pancake batter should be mixed in a blender to ensure the lightest, fluffiest pancakes in the world.

"When fat and ugly team up, stupid usually isn't too far behind." This is one of Stan's favorite "Bob-isms," while I know my mother is cringing right now that her husband's insensitivity toward annoying people has been exposed.

Get to an airport early – very early. A trip goes a lot more smoothly when it begins with a cup of coffee or cocktail at the gate; instead of a luggage-laden sprint through the terminal.

Any man who will not come to the door and introduce himself is not going to date his daughter. I wasn't allowed to leave the house in response to a honked car horn out front. I hated that rule while growing up, but now it makes all the sense in the world. And I've come to find out that Stan's dad had the same rule for his sister.

Our family is not a democracy. It is a monarchy, and Dad is king, and yes, there are double standards when it comes to rules and life is not fair, because…

"Boys have sex; girls have babies."

Never drive with the oil light on. Ever.

"Does this FEEL like an A paper?" he would ask us when proofreading a term paper. (And when he asked that, it really didn't feel like an A paper, but of course, he already knew that.)

Anyone who has to buy Lycra Spandex in size XXL should not be wearing Lycra Spandex.

Find a man who will make me the most important part of his life. (I did.)

"Nothing good happens after 1 a.m." While I fought this tooth and nail during unending curfew arguments, I eventually came to realize he was right. Then again, good and fun are not always the same thing.

Pre-tax money and compounding interest are good things, so start a 401(k) as soon as possible. (I did.)

If a girl can change a tire, she will never be stuck on the side of a road waiting for a stranger to help. (I can.)

If you don't do the little jobs well, no one will trust you with the big ones. (This was my brother's submission – after the traffic circle lesson, which topped both of our lists.)

Auctions and yard sales are great fun, even though my mom and brother are horrified by the thought of owning someone else's stuff.

Always go straight to the top, when complaining or complimenting a large corporation.

Always keep jumper cables in your trunk.

When asked for your weight before boarding a tiny plane, always add

76

about 200 pounds to your own, to make up for all the women in front of you who lied.

No guy will ever love me as much as my dad (or mom). Stan won points by acknowledging this when he asked my dad for my hand in marriage. Lucky for me, he comes a very close second, and that's all either of my parents has ever wanted.

Happy Father's Day, Dad. You and Mom really are the smartest people I know.

HOUSE RULES

I broke one of my family's cardinal rules a few weeks ago when I failed to call home on the designated evening.

Ever since my brother left for college three years before my own departure, my parents have asked only that their children check in with a phone call on Sunday evenings.

They wisely knew they wouldn't necessarily want to hear whatever was happening in the background of our dorm rooms and apartments if they happened to call on a random Thursday night, so the "Sunday call" routine was firmly established around 1991, when Kevin headed to Pace University in New York. It has remained on the books throughout the ensuing 20 years, continuing through graduations, relocations, marriages and grandchildren.

Our spouses were quickly indoctrinated to the "Sunday call" during our courtship, and both have adapted admirably, offering occasional reminders and serving as alternates when Kevin is on a business trip or I am covering an event.

The rule has remained amazingly intact through 20 years and an estimated 1,040 Sundays. Yes, there have been occasional slip-ups; usually (all right, always) mine. They either involve a guilty, but futile, too-late realization around 11:30 p.m., or a blissful unawareness of my faux pas – until the Monday morning email arrives, dripping with sarcasm, from my father.

"Can we assume our only daughter is alive and well since we didn't hear from her last night?"

"Your poor mother was up all night, sitting by a phone that didn't ring. Can she now go to sleep, secure in the knowledge that her only daughter is all right, or should she continue calling the area hospitals?"

Yada yada. (Note: Please don't envision my mother as a frail, elderly woman sitting fretfully with a hand on her heart. On fall Sundays, my parents are contentedly reading newspapers, grading student papers and watching football with snacks, wine and vodka tonics. They're fine. They're also the first people we call in real emergencies, because they're damn good at handling everything Kevin and I (mostly I) have thrown at them in the past few decades.

Those thankfully few emergencies actually led to an addendum to the "Sunday call rule." Once firmly established, we'd all suffer a minor cardiac event whenever someone was calling in the middle of the week. That sense of dread led to what I call the "Reassurance Rule," which requires immediate assurance that everything is fine, even before the proper greeting.

Every non-Sunday phone conversation among family members starts with, "Hey Dad, it's me, everything's fine."

"Good, what's up?" he says as his heart returns to its normal rhythm.

It's a good rule, and one that has never been broken, as far as I know. In fact, I actually got a bit carried away with it once when I was in the hospital around 1 a.m. awaiting an emergency appendectomy for a ruptured appendix and the resulting, potentially fatal, peritonitis.

Once the diagnosis had been made and the surgery scheduled, I figured the situation had become serious enough to warrant a call home, a call that I started with the usual, "Hey, it's me, everything's fine, but....."

What can I say? Old habits die hard. Just like some of the other long-standing rules in our family:

When splitting the last piece of cake or anything else, one person cuts and the other person chooses their half.

The tattletale gets the same punishment as the offender.

Lock your bike. This one applies not just to family, but to anyone who stays at our shore house and borrows any of the myriad bikes in the garage.

Return your seasonal beach tag at the end of your stay in Ocean City. Failure to do so may result in fines and a prohibition on future visits.

No dogs on the furniture. This applied to our mutt, Sneakers, but was regularly broken by her and by me. There were plenty of nights I'd let her into bed with me, with the unspoken agreement that she'd be back on the floor when my alarm went off.

You are, under no circumstances, to attract the attention of the seagulls or the lifeguards when consuming a deli sandwich and contraband beer on the beach. The beers are to be clinked as quietly as possible during transfer to red, plastic cups, and the sandwiches are to remain low at your side, preferably covered by your other hand. After all these years, I can't figure out why we don't just bring cans of beer to avoid the clink of glass and save space in the cooler with the crushed empties.

Once again, old habits die hard. And one of them will find me on the front porch this evening, dialing the most familiar number of my life – and swearing I won't screw it up again next week.

roboneal.com

THIRTY YEARS AGO

Thirty years ago, a businessman was born. He was born at the Jersey Shore but destined for places like White Plains, Manhattan, Raleigh and Connecticut and Boston.

He cheated in Monopoly from the time he was old enough to read the Community Chest cards and calculate 10 percent of the luxury tax bill. He hid money under the board and regaled me with the advantages of owning all four railroads – while he built hotels on the yellow and green properties and tried to convince others that two hotels were allowed, and whoever landed on it paid twice the highest rent shown on the property deed.

He gave me the crappy ship when we played with his Star Wars figures in the basement in Kansas City. I had to use some sand-colored hovercraft that wasn't allowed to fly any higher than my 3-year-old knees. He manned the Millennium Falcon and the Death Star.

He made up names for my dolls while testing their aerodynamics, and laughed when my Rubik's Cube Halloween costume got me stuck during the school parade and prevented me from putting my hands together.

He tickled me until I wet my pants, and told me to hang onto our automatic garage door opener while he pushed the button to make it rise; but never told me to let go before the door reached the top and I landed in an unceremonious heap on the driveway.

He always won the breaking of the wishbone after Thanksgiving and found the most Easter eggs in the backyard. He changed the rules in card games he taught me so he would always win and gave me wet willies in the backseat on long trips.

But...

He also tried to teach me to drive a stick shift on his Jeep in the parking lot at a local synagogue. He let me spend weekends with him at college when I was just a lowly high school student, but kept his friends and roommates away from me.

He taught me algebra and geometry over the phone from his college dorm and picked me up from parties without telling our parents where I actually had been. He provided hours of entertainment by getting so drunk after work in the summer that he pedaled his bike into the garage before opening the garage door, and then passed out on my bathroom floor.

He spelled "duet" in a sixth-grade spelling bee "d-u-t-e" while trying to impress the new teacher. He let me walk the new puppy in the wet grass of our Omaha backyard, and then saved my life when the dog yanked me to the curb and wrapped me around the mailbox.

He gave me free pork roll sandwiches from his perch on the Ocean City boardwalk, and helped me splatter paint my bedroom while mom and dad were out of town.

He dug the biggest holes on the beach using only a clam shell, and sometimes let me use his Boogie board rather than my simply ineffective blue and white Styrofoam belly board.

He covered for me and wrote down my contact information when I took unannounced trips to places like New Orleans or Tucson. He never told dad.

He stood in a tiny, hot classroom in a North Carolina college to watch me graduate (although in fairness, I sat in a hot, crowded gym to watch him do the same.) And he's rolled his eyes while handing me money in a

Washington, D.C. bar to buy the next round of drinks.

He introduced me to my nephew (although I should also thank Pam for most of that.)

He's worked for IBM, Taylor Pork Roll, a movie theater, boardwalk arcade, the Philadelphia Inquirer and Johnson's Electric.

Thirty years ago, a businessman was born at the Shore. Twenty-seven years ago that little Republican became a big brother – and it's one job he's never outgrown.

Although Monopoly will forever be out of the question, I'll always beat him at Scrabble.

Happy 30th, Kevin. I love you!

A LIFE WELL LIVED

It's strange the things we remember.

My grandmother had a huge tent party in her backyard when I was 3 or 4. I don't recall the occasion or the guest of honor, although it was probably Gram herself, as she never shied away from throwing herself a party.

But I do remember trying unsuccessfully to shimmy up the tent's supporting poles with three of my cousins. Our hands kept slipping until one of us recalled the trick Olympic gymnasts use to grip the uneven bars: chalk.

Of course, we didn't have access to any gymnast chalk, but there was always a container of scented face powder on the back of Gram's toilet that likely would have the same affect.

It did. And it sent clouds of perfumed powder into the backyard until Gram realized what had happened. She was only mildly amused, but we were immediately forgiven for the mess in both the yard and the bathroom.

Gram didn't "do" messes. She was meticulous in life, and in death, which occurred Wednesday afternoon (Dec. 16, 2009). Catherine Donnelly Bolen died in her sleep at the age of 99, and no one was ever more prepared. She had written her own obituary about six years ago. She knew what clothing she would wear to greet St. Peter, and she had the funeral Mass planned to the letter, although she likely muttered under her breath while considering the individual shortcomings of each parish priest.

Gram was ready to be reunited with her husband, my Pop, and all the other friends and family members who had made it to the Pearly Gates first. Of course, she probably headed off immediately to get her hair done before joining some heavenly bridge group.

But my Gram wasn't the typical golf, bridge, church type of lady. Yes, she enjoyed them all. But though she was only five feet tall, she was feisty and opinionated; and not always feisty in a cutesy, amusing way.

She had cocktails every afternoon with my parents – always accompanied by a snack. She carried a tiny walking stick with a ladybug handle, and she drove her electric wheelchair at dangerous speeds until a high-speed collision with a boardwalk bench curtailed her driving privileges.

She had the largest jewelry cabinet a young girl had ever seen, and she never flinched when that tiny girl adorned herself with every bead and bauble it contained.

She waited until her late 20s to marry the man of her dreams. Such a long wait was unheard of in her generation, and she privately reassured her youngest granddaughter that being single at age 30 was not only OK, but a badge of honor and a sign of independence and strength. And when I finally introduced her to the man of my dreams a few years ago, she nodded knowingly and smiled approvingly.

Gram kept her own house in perfect order until her mid-90s when she finally asked my parents if she could move across the street and live with them. They didn't hesitate to welcome her – and her unrelenting schedule – into our house.

She bought her own computer at age 91 and corresponded via e-mail with her nine grandchildren.

She protested vehemently when I playfully called her "old lady," but always pressed a secret 40 bucks into my hand when I waltzed through the kitchen.

She loved the slot machines in Atlantic City. She loved her afternoon cocktails and early dinners at the Crab Trap. She loved dessert after dinner, and taught each grandchild how to build the perfect ice cream, hot fudge and butterscotch parfait using the "fancy" glasses in the back of her cabinet and the long, twisted spoons.

She let all nine of us take her golf cart out for joyrides until the management of the retirement community passed a new policy (not based solely on the Bolen kids. There were other loud and reckless grandchildren in the neighborhood.)

Ninety-nine years were enough for Gram, but those she left behind would love just a few more days – a few more opinions and a few more parfaits. But even those wouldn't be enough, so we're content with our memories of a life well lived and a woman adored.

We bid her farewell as she brings our love to Pop. Godspeed, Gram. We'll always love you, old lady.

WE FOUND THE RIGHT RECIPE FOR THIS HOLIDAY

Welcome to the holiday season. It bustled into town while I was sorting through turkeys at Albertsons and fighting for the last roasting pan at Ross. I suppose in this season of warmth and goodwill I should apologize to the woman in the wheelchair who made the mistake of reaching for the same roasting pan during my final hours of Thanksgiving preparations. Her neck brace must have prevented her turning to see the crazed blonde stampeding down the aisle.

Yes, Christmas is less than four weeks away and will soon require our attention. But for now I'm still savoring the memories of a perfect Thanksgiving with the people who make me the happiest – and most thankful – girl in the world.

This was the first holiday meal I've ever hosted, and I have to say we nailed it even if the days leading up to this milestone meal weren't necessarily pretty.

In the end, the turkey was juicy, the pies were homemade and I got to spend the weekend with my husband and my parents, who walked us through every step of the process. After 40 Thanksgivings, many with more than 20 people around the table, they've mastered the art of food, family and alcohol.

My dad made sure my stuffing made the house smell as good as his does, and my mom expertly calculated the timing of everything while mashing potatoes, assembling a green bean casserole, pouring drinks and keeping up with dirty dishes. And she did all this while keeping up a running conversation and without ever snapping at anyone. It was extraordinary to watch.

While these miracles were happening in my kitchen, I finally found the button that ejects the beaters from the electric mixer I got as a wedding present … back in April.

No seriously, I contributed slightly more than that, and a day earlier had made my great-grandmother's apple pie recipe from scratch, crust included. Granted, the kitchen was covered in enough flour to rival the movie set of "Scarface," with clouds of it erupting every time I moved. But the pies rocked, and more importantly, passed my dad's taste test.

I can't take credit for the ultra-moist turkey that came out of the oven at exactly 5:30. I simply watched as my dad rinsed and dried the 14-pound bird that had a terrible holiday. Then Stan took over and sealed the bird in an oven roasting bag with some herbs and vegetables before enduring three hours of good-natured ribbing from his father-in-law, who repeatedly warned against the perils of a dry turkey. By the time the first few slices of meat hit the carving platter, my dad was asking for the recipe.

Dinner was served, pictures were taken and wineglasses were refilled and clinked in appreciation of good food and close families.

By 8 p.m. the dishwasher was humming with the first load and the four of us were digesting in front of a football game.

We did it. Thanksgiving was perfect.

But as I said, the days leading up to it were significantly less idyllic.

I was working, grocery shopping and cleaning everything I had ignored until company was scheduled to arrive. By the time I finished dusting every slat of the wooden window blinds, I was officially over it.

Every home improvement project we had planned since signing the lease in May was crammed into a three-day period.

Stan installed a pole across the back deck and then hung curtains to hide the tool storage area. He wrenched his back while scrubbing an area rug, and then moved furniture in the guest room. He hung fishing rod racks from the ceiling, and was nearly decapitated when I accidentally turned on the ceiling fan instead of the light while he was hanging 28 rods.

By the time my parents landed at noon on Thanksgiving Day, I was just thankful he hadn't asked for a divorce. On the contrary, he bought me roses when dispatched to the grocery store for last-minute appetizers, and constantly reassured me that all would be well.

Of course he was right. Things went even better than hoped, and I was once again reminded of how lucky I am. Not because the potatoes stayed warm or the turkey timer "popped" at the right time.

The turkey could have tasted like sandpaper, the pies could have been inedible and the rolls charred. But none of it would have mattered, because as I looked around the table last Thursday night, I knew I had everything I'll ever need.

I just hope the old lady managed to unlock her wheelchair brakes and find another roasting pan in time for her own Thanksgiving.

Happy holiday season, Key West.

NO LONGER DREAMING OF A WHITE CHRISTMAS

It was at least partially Stan's fault.

My husband had never experienced a white Christmas, and he was hoping against hope that our holiday in Boston would be the type Bing Crosby has been dreaming about for 50 years.

It worked, and 19 inches later, our flight home had been cancelled, Stan was shoveling the driveway with my brother and I was nursing a bruised tailbone and giant lump on my head. Naturally, I was the first to fall on ice, and naturally, it was entirely my own fault.

There were tire tracks down the driveway that had frozen over to a slippery strip of blacktop. Stan and I were playing around, sliding down the strip, and seeing how far we could make it. Like an idiot, I followed his advice to "get a running start up in the snow."

Then the inevitable happened.

I was about to break our own records for speed and distance when things went horribly wrong. I lost my balance and started that flailing, quick backward two-step that everyone knows is going to end in disaster; it's just a matter of how long it takes.

It didn't take me long at all, and I went down hard, landing on my tailbone and then banging my head on the cement – never a dull moment.

I once again found myself wondering how people live in a place that requires a whole separate "mud room" for cold-weather clothes and boots. My brother has a snow plow guy on retainer who comes by every three inches, and a 50-pound of Ice Away in the garage.

While tugging snow pants over boots and tightening my sleeve cuff around my glove, I wondered what had become of my previous vow to avoid all this outerwear unless there were skis on my feet and a hot tub at the bottom.

Instead, Stan and I braved the cold for a sledding session in the front yard, where I, of course, managed a perfect face plant in the snow when I overshot the sled.

Back inside, we learned we couldn't get a flight out of Boston or New Jersey until New Year's Eve, and the woman on the phone was not particularly sympathetic. Apparently, we weren't the only people stranded by a snowstorm and offering our first-born child for a seat on a southbound plane.

That's when we made a decision: road trip.

My parents, who absolutely rock, by the way, were planning to give us their Volkswagen Passat when they got a new car. Stan and I were going to fly up in January and drive it home to Key West.

The snow storm changed that itinerary and we rode from Boston to Jersey with my parents in their new car, and the next day climbed into our new, heated leather seats and pointed the car south – for two days, nine states and a small hash brown incident after the Burger King breakfast drive-thru somewhere in south Georgia.

It was a minor issue, and I'm almost positive that I found all the ones that cascaded out of the bag while Stan was pulling back onto the highway.

On a brighter note, I mastered the map and re-folded it perfectly several times. I didn't get frustrated and make my own creases, and I didn't lose my patience and just cram the thing into the backseat. But I never did figure out why a map of the southeastern United States also included Michigan and Illinois.

I also couldn't figure out why Econo Lodges don't provide conditioner in their bathrooms. We had the pleasure of staying in these lovely establishments twice in five days. We spent the night in Fort Lauderdale before the morning fight to Boston, and we slept in another Econo Lodge somewhere around the Georgia/Florida line.

One front desk guy handed me some body lotion when I asked for conditioner, so I don't know what I expected when I called the front desk asking that a courtesy tube of toothpaste be sent to Room 201. The man didn't know what toothpaste was, but at least he didn't give me anymore lotion.

But we made it.

Stan got his white Christmas, we got to spend some extra time in the freezing north, and there's a new car in our driveway.

While we take down the holiday decorations this week, we're left with a small mountain of presents, a camera full of memories and maybe one stray hash brown.

All in all, life is good and 2011 is off to a great start. But if Stan wishes for a white Christmas next year, it's over.

CAN WE KEEP HIM?

I had no idea a cat could look disappointed.

I swear I saw the one who lives at our house sigh and shake his head last week when I opened the back door and saw him in his usual spot on the deck. I think he even rolled his eyes when I asked if he was hungry and shook the bowl I had just filled with cat food.

Stan, on the other hand, is greeted with happy prancing, head rubs against his legs and a look that can only be described as awe every time he opens the back door.

Me, not so much.

In fact, three days after Stan left for an 11-week fishing trip in the Bahamas, I was treated to a dead rat at the back door, courtesy of our four-legged "Buddy." And just this week it was a bird, also dead, also by the back door.

I'm doing my best, you ungrateful beast, really I am.

Dead animals notwithstanding, I think our relationship is steadily improving, but I may need some guidance from you cat people out there.

I'm a dog person. More specifically, I'm a big-dog person and have never had much time for anything smaller than a beagle. So I wasn't overly impressed when the giant cat started showing up on our back porch two months ago, even if he is about the size of a beagle. But he became increasingly difficult to ignore as he sauntered right up (usually to Stan) and rubbed his head on our shins before climbing hesitantly onto a nearby lap, or trying to, because he doesn't necessarily fit on normal-sized thighs.

This cat is enormous – an estimated 16 pounds of long, soft fur, a sweeping tail and a tiny head with velvety cheeks. When he rubs his head against a chair or table leg, the whole thing moves across the porch.

Stan immediately won the cat's undying devotion by serving up a twice-daily feast of fresh fish – and by letting him inside and onto the couch during a thunderstorm.

I made a pretense of rolling my eyes and complaining about this denizen of our back porch that ignored me and loved my husband, but our tolerance of each other eventually gave way to begrudging affection. We bonded, I suppose.

Assuming this friendly beast was someone's lost pet, we dutifully wallpapered the neighborhood with "Found Cat" signs – before we knew it's technically illegal to post such signs on city property. We were hoping to reunite a frantic owner with this well-adjusted kitty, who was making himself quite comfortable on South Street.

A week passed before Stan got a call from the woman who had inherited the cat six years earlier when she moved into a house about three blocks away. I watched Stan's face fall as she accurately described the mouthy beast we called Buddy.

He gave the lady our address, then moped out back to say his sad good-byes. By then, even I was sad to see the cat go. He had nudged his way into our lives and home, using his freakishly strong head to skillfully squeeze through the back door before we closed it, gaining happy entrance to air-conditioned comfort – and helping himself to my seat on the couch.

Upon arrival, the cat's owners were bewildered that Buddy, whom they called Frogo, had migrated down South Street to our fenced-in backyard. Apparently, he was mainly an outdoor cat over there as well and just showed up regularly for breakfast and dinner.

The woman carried an obliging Buddy/Frogo back to her house around 7 p.m. after we had bid him a reluctant farewell.

That cat was back on our porch moving furniture around four hours later.

Stan was jubilant. I, too, was happy to see our Buddy; more so for the smile he put on my husband's face, but also because he's pretty damn lovable in his own, demanding way.

I did let the owner know "Frogo" was safe and welcome to hang out whenever he pleased. He can leap our 8-foot fence in a single bound, and so makes his neighborhood rounds, apparently helping himself to any snacks proffered on his route. But the promise of fresh fish on our back porch and the chance to spend an occasional hour inside has made our house a semi-permanent residence.

Stan's departure for the Bahamas last month had both of them concerned. My husband worried Buddy would abandon us if the gourmet cuisine of fresh fish was replaced permanently by dry Purina, so he left a bag of fish in the freezer marked "BUDDY" in big letters.

The fish ran out a week ago. Buddy enjoyed his last meal of dolphin and proceeded to turn into a teen-aged girl; rolling his eyes, sighing with frustration and storming off in a huff when I offered a bowl of dry food. If the cat had thumbs, he'd have been furiously texting his friends. If he had a middle finger, I know I would have seen it.

I think my attempted switch from Purina to dollar-store cat food was the final insult. The initial dead rat could have been a fluke. But I'm convinced the bird was left to spite me. And it worked. The next day Buddy enjoyed a salmon dinner, courtesy of Fancy Feast, and he licked the bowl clean.

The once-daily canned-food supplement to the bowl of Purina (yes, we're back to the name brand) seems to have mollified this furry interloper for the time being. He's back to rubbing against my legs and purring while he hangs off my lap.

The beast is once again our Buddy – but it's no secret that we're both counting the days until Stan comes home.

Maybe that'll wipe the disappointed look off his face.

DOGS LOVE US; CATS ENDURE US

The golden retriever at the gas station last week had never met me. I had no food, treats or tennis ball, yet the happily panting dog, standing patiently next to her owner, eagerly snuffled my outstretched hand and then ducked her soft head underneath it to ensure a quick pat of affection. The owner looked back from where she was paying at the register and smiled distractedly, clearly accustomed to these minor delays in their daily errands.

The two-second encounter brightened my day – and the dog's – just a little.

Ten minutes later I crossed our front porch carrying a bag of cat food and a packet of tuna-flavored treats and received nothing but a blank stare and a single, slow blink from the giant cat that decided to make our house his last year.

This is my first cat, and no one told me not to expect much.

I grew up with a big, lovable mutt named Sneakers. She'd fall all over herself to greet anyone who came to the door and trot innocently into the family room with a spaghetti noodle dangling from one ear, convinced her after-dinner foray into the garbage can was still a covert operation.

She wasn't going to lead any blind people through downtown intersections, and she couldn't sniff out bombs, drugs or bodies. But she could hear the slightest ding of the cookie jar from two floors below. She knew the route that led to the vet and panicked when a typically thrilling car ride fell apart with a particular left turn. She knew which friends let themselves in the back door and which meter readers were undoubtedly serial killers – until they got down on one knee and offered the same greeting I gave the golden last week.

Dogs in general are absurdly happy to see, well, anyone – except the vet, of course. Their faces light up when they make eye contact with any stranger who looks like a candidate for affection.

Cats, not so much.

Oh sure, they'll saunter up and rub against your legs, or knock their head coyly against your hand while you're trying to pour food into the bowl without spilling it all over the kitchen, but the affection from a cat is always on their own terms.

Anyone who grew up with a dog will understand my puzzlement at a cat that stands three feet away, staring and yawning at your outstretched hand. Maybe he'll deign to close the distance and wander over, maybe not. Maybe he'll just keep standing there, waiting to see how desperate you get for his attention.

It's the same with food. Cats are snobs.

Dogs don't even taste half the food they accept from strangers. They're just so happy to be offered anything other than Purina Dog Chow that they inhale the bite of hamburger – or the doggie pill buried in a smear of peanut butter atop a Ritz cracker.

Cats just sniff tentatively at whatever's offered before walking stiffly away.

Granted, in terms of evolution and survival of the fittest, cats, with their innate skepticism and staunch judgments, would surely do better than dogs. But in terms of overall happiness, dogs have it all figured out. Their enthusiasm is contagious. A happily panting dog can bring a business-suited professional to his knees and have him rolling around the carpet with one excited lick.

A cat just watches silently while we move from our chair to the floor and ultimately end up crawling to them, only to get a close-up view of their upraised tail as they turn and walk away. But as soon as the cat is ready for affection, they're happy to scare the hell out of us by springing onto the cushion behind our head and then start clenching and un-clenching those razor sharp claws on a beach towel, blanket or my thigh – whichever is closer.

My friend, Sheila, wrote to me last year when Buddy first showed up – on our back porch and in this column. She passed on an observation that cat people have apparently known for some time: Dogs have owners; cats have staff.

It's true. Dogs will do anything to win us over; cats just watch unim-pressed as we enthusiastically beckon, nod and make kissing sounds while tapping the seat next to us. I swear Buddy rolls his eyes every time he walks away from one of our attempts to impress him with a piece of string tied to a balled-up sock.

As if that's not bad enough, I've now become one of those people who write about their cat. What's next, a gleeful fit whenever Stan jangles the car keys and a spaghetti noodle dangling from my ear?

A CAVALIER ATTITUDE

This time I said good-bye.

We'd spent the past 10 years and five months together; we'd shared long drives, Saturdays filled with short errands, favorite songs with the windows down, days at the beach and stormy nights when the repetition of the windshield wipers and that moment of silence under a highway overpass were the only comforts.

But it all ended Monday morning when I handed the keys of my old, maroon Saturn to a complete stranger in exchange for $1,200. It seemed like such a callous transaction, but I was able to tap her on the hood, where the paint is peeling and wish her well.

It was the end of an era that began right around my high school graduation. But back then, I didn't have a chance to say good-bye to the Plymouth station wagon that had been my first car. The new Saturn was a surprise from my parents, so the blue wagon was already gone by the time I inhaled the Saturn's new car smell.

I think the old "grocery getter" still had one of my ponytail holders around the gear shift and an R.E.M. tape stuck in the unreachable abyss between the seat and the center console when they left it at the dealership.

Sure, I regretted not saying a proper farewell, but come on, I was 18 and there was a brand new car beckoning. No sense standing around blubbering over a station wagon that smelled like our dog.

Last weekend, almost 11 years later, a new car once again beckoned; well, new to me, at least. Thanks to my 94-year-old grandmother and her decision (mandate) to stop driving her Mercedes, I ended up with the 98' Chevy Cavalier that was my mom's until Sunday afternoon. Mom got the Mercedes and I got her Cavalier Rally Sport with new tires, brakes and other things fathers deem important when donating a car to their daughter. My parents got the proceeds from the sale of my Saturn.

My new used car has power windows, power brakes, power locks and only two pedals; no more charley horses from the clutch while sitting in traffic on North Roosevelt Boulevard.

As you may know, I'm from New Jersey, as are my grandmother, my parents and their vehicles. Enter Dad, the super hero who could always raise my bike seat to the right height, teach me how to not throw like a girl and ensure that I could navigate the Garden State's hazardous traffic circles that have baffled Pennsylvania drivers for decades.

Of course, those navigation lessons usually included my father bracing himself with a stiff right arm against the dashboard while his right foot stomped uselessly through the floorboards of the passenger side seeking the non-existent brake. His left hand wiped the sweat out of his eyes, which were alternately clenched shut or wide open as his life flashed before them.

And let's not forget the yelling – because it's always easier for a 17-year-old to avoid other cars, stay in the outside lane and exit the circle smoothly while the man in the passenger seat screams a dizzying combination of orders, profanity and Hail Mary's.

Amazingly, I've mastered the circles (of course that's my opinion, not necessarily my Dad's), can change a tire, raise my own bike seat and make an accurate throw from home plate to second base.

I also can get into the air-conditioned comfort of my new Cavalier today because my dad left Ocean City, N.J. at 5 a.m. Saturday and headed south on I-95. He was going to stop somewhere south of Jacksonville, but NASCAR races and hurricane victims had filled all hotels between Daytona and Fort Lauderdale. So he drove straight through to Fort Lauderdale, where I was to meet him at noon on Sunday.

He then bought me lunch on Las Olas Boulevard and a drink at a beach bar before boarding a plane headed for home.

I'm really glad I got the chance to say good-bye to my beloved Saturn, but I'm happier to have said hello to the world's greatest dad in Fort Lauderdale – where there are no traffic circles.

RUMORS OF MY PREGNANCY ARE GREATLY EXAGGERATED

I heard from a friend Thursday evening that I was pregnant.

The news came as a complete shock, especially since I was on my way to the bar at an art show opening. It also made me rethink the three vodka drinks I had had the previous night, and do some quick math, considering my husband has been out of the country for nine weeks.

Nope, the pregnancy rumor is not true, so anyone else who's heard it needs to correct it as soon as possible. I don't want everyone in town staring judgmentally at me every time I order a coffee, a cocktail or raw fish.

We haven't decided on kids yet, although I have no doubt Stan would be a terrific father. There are no doubts – only hope for the possibilities that would come with a daughter.

I hope she climbs onto his lap in her pajamas after a nighttime bath so he can blow dry her hair without pulling on the tangles.

I hope he strains his back running up and down the sidewalk holding onto the seat of her new two-wheeler.

I hope he spends hours in the backyard with a baseball to make sure she doesn't throw like a girl.

I hope he gets whiplash while teaching her to drive a stick shift.

I hope he quizzes her on her science chapter the night before a test.

I hope he proofreads her book reports. (Oh wait, that was always Mom, and would also be my job, as the writer in the house.)

I hope he slips her some cash every time she visits.

I hope he goes to every basketball, softball and field hockey game, even if he doesn't understand field hockey, and even if she doesn't get much playing time.

I hope he takes her and her friends to a fancy steak dinner for her Sweet 16.

I hope he makes thin, fluffy pancakes every Christmas morning.

I hope he teaches her his favorite folk songs and then dances to their favorite at her wedding 30 years later.

I hope that someday she'll be able to let him know how much she loves him.

I hope they share an indescribable bond between a dad and his little girl.

And I hope our little girl's grandfather knows that he made it all possible.

Well, he and her grandmother, my mom, who, by the way, did just as much and was by our side for all the above-described activities.

Hallmark needs to create a Parents' Day, because while I'll always be Daddy's Little Girl, neither of us would be anything without my mom.

Happy Father's Day, Dad and Mom.

(But not yet to Stan, I swear.)

HOMEWARD BOUND

Thomas Wolfe said you can't do it.

But Jon Bon Jovi, in his latest Jersey/country persona, seems to think it's possible.

"It doesn't matter where you are, doesn't matter where you go
If it's a million miles away or just a mile up the road
Take it in, take it with you when you go, who says you can't go home."

So I'm doing it this weekend — goin' home.

Yes, it will be cold and a little bleak at the Jersey Shore in November. Yes, the boardwalk funnel cake stands and amusement rides will be shuttered and empty. The seagulls will be tossed around in the wind, and the beach chairs will be stacked in the garage for another year.

But it's home and some things never change at that 100-year-old house on Park Place.

I'm no longer the youngest person in most family photos and the faded inflatable raft in the garage isn't big enough to make me float.

But the second step after the landing still squeaks in the middle but not at the edges, and the door to the third floor still groans upon opening and closing. But a magazine shoved near the hinge still works to avoid the noise (and the sharp ears of anyone trying to figure out what time someone else went to bed.)

The kitchen has been redone a few times since I was a little girl, and I still habitually open the cabinet that held the cereal bowls 15 years ago, but another cabinet still – and always will – hold Pop Tarts and peanut butter.

The combination to the padlock on the detached garage has not changed in 15 years, and if it ever does the entire neighborhood will need to be alerted to the new combination. The big trash cans in the alley behind the house still have our house number, 822, painted on them to avoid summertime trashcan thieves, and my mom is still convinced that stray cats wander into the downstairs laundry room if the door is not closed.

The same metal grate has covered the drain next to the outside shower since my parents were teen-agers, and the door to the second-floor linen closet still swells and sticks in the humidity so you have to tap the top of the door it to open it. The inside of that little closet will always smell like the Shore.

I know exactly how hot the water gets in the old sinks with separate faucets for hot and cold water and the rubber stopper to fill the sink with warm water is still connected by the same old chain. The hidden key has been on the same nail under the same step since I was sneaking in after curfew and avoiding the second-step squeak.

The same banister has held Christmas stockings for decades and every grandchild has been entertained for hours by the cuckoo clock in the kitchen. The same board acts as a lock when it's laid behind the sliding glass door. The chips are in the same drawer, the liquor is on the same top shelf and the phone list on the refrigerator still lists family, friends, the deli around the corner and the best pizza place on the boardwalk.

The same crack in the same sidewalk is still breaking mothers' backs and the same mom always knows what time you get home — always.

More than the closets, cracks, creaks and clocks, it's the people around the kitchen table, on the front porch and in the living room that make the old house our home. The same parents worry about the same kids. The same friends use the back door and enter without knocking. The same relatives bring the same dramas that are dissected after they leave and the same family sticks together.

You really can go home.

Bon Jovi wouldn't lie.

LOVE STORIES

MY VALENTINE IS EVERY DAY

Before we get started, let me just say that the painting project last week was an unparalleled success. The living room is a soothing green and the woodwork is gleaming white. We were finished in time for the Super Bowl kickoff and are still on speaking terms.

I'd be lying if I said there weren't a few setbacks, which are obvious from the new green spots on the carpet, but things could've gone much worse. For example, when my left heel somehow caught the edge of my paint tray (swear to God), most of the color landed on my foot, ankle and calf rather than the carpet. And although we both were carefully navigating the living room obstacle course and staying on the drop cloth, I was the only one who kept getting paint on the bottom of one foot and making three small toe prints before realizing the problem.

Nevertheless, we're truly pleased with the results — and actually had a good time doing it.

Now, moving on to today's scribbling … it's Valentine's Day, that silly commercial holiday that puts ridiculous pressure on otherwise happy couples, and often makes single people feel like crap. It's a terrible holiday, and the horror starts in elementary school when kids grab for the limited supply of red and pink construction paper to make an envelope that will hold the store-bought valentine cards from classmates. The little envelopes may also contain a few of those chalky heart candies asking a 6-year-old to "Be Mine."

As I sit writing this, I'm looking at my own Valentine's Day roses that were lovingly handed over a few days early to be sure I got the biggest and brightest and so I could enjoy them all weekend.

They make me smile for so many reasons, and they all have everything to do with the man who bought them.

I smile because he spent all day Friday under my car replacing the motor on my radiator fan, and because he loaned me his truck for the two weeks my car was broken.

I smile because he never got frustrated when I stepped in my paint tray and walked on the carpet. He just rolled his eyes, shook his head and laughed.

I smile because he puts a cup of water on my nightstand every night, leaves a note on the coffee table every morning and always comes home from the store with a little bag of my favorite Caramel Creams.

I smile at the text message that said, "You're my world," and because he watched "Annie" with me when he learned it was a childhood favorite.

I smile because he hung 50 red bows around the house at Christmastime and played carols while he did it.

I smile because he once snuck out of a party that was only serving rum to get me a drink I enjoy. I smile because he holds my hand when we walk and asks for seconds of my cooking even when we both know it's not very good.

I smile because he traveled all the way to Jersey for just one night to ask my dad just one question about my left hand.

I don't need 12 roses on one day in February. A lifetime of laughter, love notes, caramel creams and car repairs will begin for us on the 10th day of April, and from that day forward, he'll "be mine," and I'll be his, green paint and all.

AND NOW A WORD FOR OUR SPONSORS ...

In three weeks, this column will have a new author.

I'll still be the one fretting over the keyboard late Friday or early Saturday, but the name under the photo will be different. Mandy Bolen will cease to exist around 6 p.m. on April 10.

After a few heartfelt words, a shiny new ring and an official declaration, Mandy Miles will make her entrance into this world wearing a white dress and surrounded by people who love her. Some in the crowd will have her former and familiar last name, Bolen, while others will welcome her into a new world of Miles.

Those two worlds will combine joyously amid tears, laughter, memories, music and cocktails, and I can't wait. But before the beauty of a wedding comes the ugliness of its planning, and believe me, it hasn't been pretty. If you, folks, are sick of reading about the wedding, then try planning it.

Stop by our house for a glimpse of the utter chaos that will become an unforgettable day. Tiny seashells, a bag of sand and 100 tea candles will become centerpieces. The boxes stacked in the foyer will be lovingly wrapped and distributed to bridesmaids and groomsmen. The scraps of paper stacked on the coffee table will become our wedding vows and the tiny boxes on the curio cabinet contain the rings we'll wear forever.

Everything will come together beautifully, but in the meantime is a bit all-consuming, so please bear with me for another three weeks. This ordeal has tested my already-questionable organizational skills. It has devoured my evenings and taken me to Web sites I never knew existed. Did you know you can buy tiny, personalized tins of mints to give to wedding guests? Would you know where to find a tuxedo for a ring-bearing dog? The Internet, of course, has been a valuable and intriguing resource, often for showing me things so ridiculous that I become thankful for the relative normalcy of our impending nuptials.

Along the way, I've also learned that this tiny island has the essential ingredients for the perfect start to a new life. Sure, I regularly complain about our lack of a Target, a mall and an Olive Garden, but we have the important stuff.

Location, location, location. And we picked the perfect one when we chose West Martello Tower for our wedding and reception. Operated by the Key West Garden Club, the waterfront garden is filled with flowering plants, orchids, palm trees and meandering cobblestone pathways that go through and under centuries-old banyan trees. The scenery, and the people mingling among it, will be captured in photographs by our good friend, Rob O'Neal, who will pull double-duty as photographer and groomsman. I can't thank him enough for all he's done for me in the past 11 years.

Jimmy and Joanna Cooper of Soundwave Productions will provide the music for dancing and the videography to capture the most important day of my life. Caterer extraordinaire Tami McGrail, of Sebago Yacht Catering at The Galleon, is cooking up some seriously delicious duck empanadas, shrimp quesadillas and seared tuna — and managing to make the garden look even better than usual. The Conch Tour Train will get everyone safely from the Southernmost Hotel to the garden and back again. The Southernmost will welcome nearly 100 of our guests, arriving from all over, so there should be some interesting poolside gatherings throughout the wedding week.

Phil and Kelly Cooke, new owners of The Galleon's Tiki Bar, will host our rehearsal dinner party, while Cakes by Karol is whipping up a German chocolate groom's cake for Mr. Miles. The flowers are by Gilda and expertly assembled by our friend, Josh Scaturro. The beer is from Anheuser-Busch, the vodka is from Russia and the 150 guests are from everywhere. On April 10, a Georgia boy will marry a Jersey girl with friends and family coming from each place to witness the event and perhaps restart the Civil War.

Three weeks to go – what could possibly go wrong?

roboneal.com

I DO – AND ALWAYS WILL

So this is what it feels like to wake up with a new name.

Day one of married life, and I have to say, it's wonderful. I am officially the happiest girl in the world – and the luckiest. I will never take for granted the love in my life, or the people who shower me with it.

I can't stop looking at the new ring that represents a new life; one I will build with my best friend, my husband.

It will be a life filled with big decisions and little love notes, inside jokes and secret memories. There will be arguments, apologies and a million ways to show our love.

Luckily, I have two ideal role models for a marriage that is as happy and fun as it is strong and lasting. Those unions are rare these days, so I'm glad I've been paying attention for the past 33 years.

My dad still pulls my mom unexpectedly into his lap for a quick kiss and longstanding joke. After 40 years of marriage, he still kisses her in the kitchen and tells her she's the "best lookin' girl in the world."

My mom still bakes my dad's favorite apple pie for Christmas and Thanksgiving, even though she doesn't even like pie, and always gets frustrated making the thin, flaky crust. It's the same recipe my great-grandmother used and wrote down in her distinctive penmanship when my newlywed mom spent the day in Gram Donnelly's kitchen learning the painstaking pie techniques for her new husband.

When I was a little kid, my mom spent every moment making her kids good people. But she always put on lipstick, combed her hair and "gussied up" 10 minutes before my dad got home from work.

"I like to look nice for your Dad," she told me when I was 4 and watching her apply pink lipstick while standing in the hallway of our Kansas City home.

And every winter night in New Jersey, my dad gets into bed five minutes before my mom to warm up her side.

But when he came home from a garage sale years ago as the proud owner of an antique (and troubled) MG Midget, my mom just smiled, rolled her eyes and climbed in. (She continued rolling her eyes for the next five years every time the car broke down.)

A few years ago, my parents bought a tandem bike for whimsical rides on the boardwalk. (I'll admit, they rarely ride it, and I believe there were a few choice words exchanged during the maiden voyage. But at least they liked each other enough after more than 30 years of marriage to even contemplate such a purchase.)

My folks probably never realized that I noticed all these things and countless more. To them, they weren't significant actions, just little ways to show and share their love every day.

But those little things, piled on top of each other for 40 years, became something huge, something strong – and something to emulate.

Yesterday, Stan and I made a promise in front of 150 people to start our own series of little things that will mark a lifetime of love.

Together, we'll find our own way without leaving anyone behind. I'm not taking a son, a brother and an uncle away from his family. They've welcomed me into theirs.

My brother didn't lose a sister, he gained a brother. And my parents didn't lose a daughter, they gained a son. (Although, after paying for yesterday's promise at the world's most perfect wedding, they probably wouldn't mind one less expense.)

Scores of friends and relatives filled the Key West Garden Club at West Martello to share our happiness, support our union and drink our booze. They traveled from all over to celebrate with us, and we all know this island isn't the most affordable or conveniently located weekend destination.

Cousins and friends drove from mainland airports with impatient kids and pregnant wives in tiny rental cars. They boarded pre-dawn flights and wrestled presents through security. They took time off work and bought bridesmaid dresses. They endured 15-hour road trips just so they could be here for us.

So I truly thank everyone who made the trip. (Note: I'm writing this column a few days before a wedding that has the potential to get completely out of hand, so I don't yet know if I need to add any apologies to the thank-yous. Those will come later if necessary, after today's debriefing and rehashing.)

For now, I'm just going to savor this feeling. I'll keep looking at my ring, but also at my family and my husband – who made it all possible.

No apologies were necessary following the best day of my life, but the wedding week did involve an unscheduled trip to the emergency room two days before the nuptials, when Stan broke two ribs while fishing with his best man. He was in enough pain, so I refrained from reminding him of my suggestion that he forego fishing that day and instead hang around to greet our arriving guests. He hates when I'm right.

ALL'S RIGHT WITH THE WORLD

All is right with my world again.

A second pair of sunglasses sits next to mine on the kitchen counter. There are two sets of flip-flops kicked off under the coffee table and the A/C filter is clean.

That's right, my husband's finally home.

Stan returned Wednesday after fishing a marlin tournament for 11 weeks in the Bahamas. I was at the dock at the Galleon Marina to welcome him, eager to return to our two-person household routine. I lived alone for nine years and thoroughly enjoyed it, but once you share a life, a home and a future with your best friend, being single isn't much fun.

Oh sure, we're tempted by initial tiny rebellions the first few solo nights. For instance, I may have run the dishwasher with only four plates, three cups and about eight pieces of silverware inside. I may have smoked a cigarette in the living room. I may have thrown away some leftovers. I may have ransacked his truck ashtray for quarters. And I may have tried to hang a mirror in the center of a wall without the benefit of a measuring tape, and that may have been a bad idea.

These are all just possibilities, of course; things I may have done without someone there to point out the folly of my thinking. (I admit to nothing, by the way.)

But the enjoyment derived from any of those acts can't come close to the happiness I enjoy every day after work when I see both the scooter and the truck in the driveway, knowing the presence of both means that my favorite person is inside. I still look forward to hanging out with him every evening, whether we have dinner plans at a friend's house, or no plans but the couch.

So on Wednesday night, I happily migrated back to my side of the bed. (It seems I may drift toward the middle when sleeping alone.) A gentle, 4 a.m. nudge reminded me that a queen-sized bed is designed to accommodate two people – as long as one of them is not in a diagonal sprawl with arms outstretched and three pillows strewn about.

By the time I got home from work the next day, the A/C filter was clean, there was air in the truck tires, wiper fluid for my car and laundry being gathered in the bedroom.

That's right; my husband – like my dad – does laundry. It's a beautiful thing, given my well-documented dread of the particular household task. Stan washes, I fold. It all works out – when he's in town.

I was forced to make the dreaded march myself to the laundry room in recent weeks. It sucked.

Why can't appliance manufacturers indicate on the machine how long each cycle lasts, or how much time remains in the final spin cycle? Oh sure, we all figure it out eventually and approximately, but it would eliminate those premature trips to the laundry room and the frustrated indecision that comes in deciding whether to return to the house for another five minutes, or just wait out the spin cycle while glaring at the thrumming machine.

How about a heads up on the dryer as well? How long does the initial 75 cents give you, and will the clothes be dry at that point, or do we need to budget $1.50 for that?

Oh, and anyone who is now smugly saying that the timing would vary based on the level of heat we've selected obviously does not use coin-operated dryers. Trust me, low heat is not an option when you're paying for it. Just ask anyone who's gotten second-degree burns from a pair of button-fly jeans.

Thankfully, our household routine is back on track and I can avoid the laundry room.

Unfortunately, I couldn't avoid walking past the wall with the newly installed mirror, but as I write this, Stan has a pencil in his mouth and a tape measure in his hand.

Welcome home, my love. I missed you.

MARRIAGE COMES WITH JOB DESCRIPTIONS

I don't remember anything in my wedding vows about paying bills or buying birthday cards, yet I found myself bent over the coffee table last week writing checks and stamping the appropriate return envelopes.

I realized then that I had watched my mom perform this task every month as well, except she sat at our kitchen table. I also realized I never had seen my dad or my husband dutifully writing checks and, once finished, jotting our address in the upper left corner of each envelope.

The bills are one of those household tasks that get divided between husband and wife without discussion, and as we approach our one-year anniversary, I can happily say we've gotten these things figured out.

If marriage were a corporation, I'd be Chief Executive Officer and Stan Chief Operating Officer. I handle the administrative side of things, and he oversees operations. Believe me, it's best this way. Any reversal in those roles tends to end badly.

Take for example, the recent renewal of Stan's captain's license, which had to be submitted to a Miami office by Monday. It was surely an administrative task; nightmare, actually, but it was one that he had to handle, requiring documentation from other captains about time on the water, a doctor's physical and a drug test. I did what I could by affixing a pink reminder Post It to the coffee table – a month ago. Then I printed out the necessary forms and stuck them under the Post It – a week ago.

Yet on Friday afternoon, Stan found himself running around, getting forms signed and calling the doctor's office all before FedEx closed at 6 p.m. I stepped in to help where I could, and by 5:45 he was running to FedEx – but without the address of the Miami office. I handed him the slip, shaking my head, and he was out the door, thanking me profusely for stepping into his administrative nightmare.

And these roles work in reverse as well.

Stan never vowed to make sure the tub empties properly by regularly removing a disgusting and slimy clump of hair from the drain. For one thing, it would have been unseemly to mention clogs and slime during a wedding ceremony. But it's also not his hair that slows things down.

These things just fall into the operations category. Unfortunately, when I venture into his realm, things tend to break.

Just the other day I was switching the license plate on my new car. I breezily told Stan I didn't need any help to unscrew a few bolts, grabbed a screwdriver and headed outside; only to return three second later for a Phillips heads screwdriver. Simple mistake, could have happened to anyone.

I managed to muscle the rusted screws out of position, and then brushed away a few disintegrated pieces of plastic that were behind the license plate. Surely, those weren't needed.

Aligning the holes, I found that the screws would only turn twice before getting stuck. No worries, they were in far enough and the license plate wasn't going anywhere. This is what I told Stan when I returned. He looked dubiously at me before going to investigate my handiwork in the driveway.

"See, they're attached, they won't fall off, it'll be fine," I told him brightly.

Stan then grabbed the license and wiggled it a bit, pointing out the half-inch of play that would surely have produced an annoying rattle while driving, and would eventually have worked the screws loose.

"Hmph, I can't believe your dad would have had this dangling so loosely without any spacers to secure it," my husband said, heading toward the house.

Spacers? Might those have been the round, plastic discs that I had deemed unnecessary?

Yep.

After removing the license plate and installing the spacers, the job was finished with no rattle. See? Operations.

So I'll keep paying the bills to ensure the lights stay on, the toilet flushes and the phones ring. I'll buy the birthday cards, make the doctor's appointments and handle airline reservations.

He'll change the oil, clean the A/C filters, hang the pictures, build me a new coffee table and fix everything I break.

Vows or no vows, it's just better this way.

A (MARRIED) YEAR IN REVIEW

"In this moment, I marry my best friend, and I will make my home in your heart for all the days of my life."

That moment occurred one year ago today, and those words – our wedding vows – were the most important ones I've ever written – or uttered.

We'll say them again today at the top of the hill at the Key West Garden Club. There will be no receiving line or open bar, and it won't involve my parents' checkbook.

Today will just be the two of us, hand in hand, recalling the first year of our shared lifetime.

In a word, it rocked; we rocked, and we shattered that old "expert" opinion about the first year of marriage being the most difficult. We've handled medical emergencies in third-world countries. We moved into a new house while one of us was fishing in the Bahamas, we endured cooking disasters, hosted a perfect Thanksgiving dinner and managed an unplanned road trip from Jersey to Key West after a Christmas blizzard.

Difficult? No way.

But there is a bit of a learning curve in marriage, and the past 12 months have taught me:

Turning up the radio is no longer a sufficient method of silencing a mysterious rattle in an automobile that has both our names on the insurance card. Rattles are not tolerated. Their source will be identified and silenced before conversation can resume.

Men are apparently struck by a more life-threatening strain of the common cold than women. It's the only explanation for my husband's ability to clench his teeth and simply deal with a fish hook under a fingernail. But substitute the fish hook for a stuffy nose, sore throat and slight fever, and the end is near. When men get sick their sighs are long, their tempers are short and they are sicker than anyone has ever been.

The expiration date on a milk carton is not the day the milk gets poured down the drain. Rather, the stamp represents the day a man starts smelling the milk before every pour. (It's also the day I buy a new gallon of milk and start using it; no smelling required.)

It takes my husband six and a half minutes to realize he's hot because

I have quietly adjusted the thermostat while walking through the kitchen.

Married men are finally secure enough to acknowledge that another man is attractive; as long as the attractive man is an inaccessible celebrity. For instance, my husband won't point enthusiastically to a group of fighter pilots in flight suits at the next table, but he will sweetly pause in his channel surfing for one of my celebrity crushes, saying, "There's your boy."

Conversely, I'm happy to alert him to any television appearance by Jessica Alba, Taylor Swift or Cameron Diaz, but I'm less likely to point out the little spring break chippie who's a dead ringer for one of them on Duval Street.

One can never have too many flashlights or adhesive products i.e. Super Glue, duct tape, electrical tape in three colors, wood glue, Gorilla Glue and a few types of industrial-strength epoxy.

Toothpaste lasts a week longer when it's being used by men, who spend an inordinate amount of time flattening, folding and creasing the tube to eek out every last little bit. If there's a stand-by tube in the medicine cabinet, I'll start on it while he sprains his wrist with the old one. But when there's not yet a back-up, I happily appreciate his efforts.

Men will suffer a mild panic attack watching women jam a handful of currency into a pocket or wallet without any regard for the bills' denomination or the direction they're facing. Apparently, money is supposed to be facing the same way in ascending order. Me, I prefer to be surprised by the $10 bill that's crumpled amid a clump of singles.

Aside from these minor observations, I've also learned some of the most important lessons of my life in the past 12 months:

My husband will always take my hand and guide me, knowing I can't see well in the dark.

He'll always worry when I drive alone at night, will check my oil and fill my wiper fluid.

It truly hurts him to see me upset, and he'll do everything in his power to make me feel better when I'm sick, laugh when I'm sad or smile when I don't know what else to do.

One year ago, Stan and I promised to take care of each other for the rest of our lives, and I'm lucky enough to have two parents who are still in the process of keeping the same promise they made to me almost 35 years ago.

roboneal.com

FISH TALES AREN'T ALWAYS TOLD
IN THE SAME LANGUAGE

There are times my husband speaks a language I can't understand. No it's not the typical man-woman miscommunication squabbles about what he says, and what I really mean when I ask whether he's cool enough in the 60-degree living room. And it's not the Southerner in him. I've managed to get past the "might oughta's" and "I reckons," and have even been known to utter the occasional "y'all."

It's the fisherman in him.

Stan came home from a full-day fishing charter last week, smiling and chattering, breathless as a little boy. The only thing missing from his wide-eyed narrative was the interjection of a 5-year-old's series of "and then...," "and then...."

From what I could discern, they had a great day on the water, and came home with two big wahoo, several yellowtail snapper, king mackerel and triggerfish. I congratulated him while pouring us both a glass of wine.

He said they also caught a few tilefish and snowy grouper when they "deep-dropped at the Ups and Downs using a leader with four circle hooks with a swivel at the bottom attached to a four-pound lead."

That's when he lost me.

I was still smiling and nodding encouragingly at my husband, who was putting away tackle and sharpening knives while continuing his monologue about the day's strategies, successes and some problem with the anchor line.

There was talk of small ballyhoo whose bellies were too mushy, and a perfect throw of the cast net on 11 dozen big ballyhoo with apparently stronger bellies. These were brined with ice, salt and salt water before being vacuum-packed and frozen for later use.

See? I was listening. And I caught most of what he was saying.

All right, half.

By the time Stan put a bag of grouper filets in the fridge while discussing the electric reel he set up for an older client, I was trying to remember how much mojo sauce was in the pantry and deciding between rice and baked potatoes with our fish dinner.

It's not that I'm not interested. On the contrary, I love hearing about his days on the water, the jokes on the radio and the happy chaos that ensues in the cockpit when the fish are biting, the lines are tightening and the clients are fighting (the fish, not each other.) But I also know for a fact that I'm not the only fisherman's wife whose eyes occasionally glaze over with confusion during talk of swimming-mullet teasers, leaders, mono vs. fluorocarbon, circle hooks, swivels, belly strips, schoolies, Bimini twists and Yucatan knots.

We really try, you guys. But there's a lot going on aboard those boats and inside those tackle bags. You have more colorful, rubber things in there than the condom baskets at gay bars.

We don't always know which fish like which color Storm lure, or when we should "drop back" to let a fish eat instead of setting the hook immediately.

And sometimes we make mistakes during a cast, and end up with that tangle of line you call a "bird's nest" at the end of our rod. These things happen.

We really do appreciate your patience, or at least your attempt at patience, and we know you don't always enjoy setting your own rod down to re-bait our hook or untangle our tip-wrapped line.

We also understand that you're not always hugely disappointed when we decide not to accompany you to the fishing pier on a beautiful evening when the wind lays down and the water clears up.

I realize that watching me cast a line hurts Stan as much it hurts me to watch him type.

Now that I think about it, he doesn't fully understand how the newsroom works, and his eyes occasionally glaze over when my colleagues and I talk about story slugs, budget lines, cut lines, attribution, leads and sources.

But he's interested and supportive. He always listens to my newspaper talk, and he follows the office gossip that I share each night.

So I suppose it's a good thing that we're each in the right line of work, doing something we truly enjoy.

I may someday learn enough to be a good fisherman, but probably not. He may someday be able to type more than 12 words a minute, but probably not.

In the meantime, we'll both keep doing what we love and will keep listening to everything each other says – well, most of it.

All right, half. (By the way, we had plenty of mojo, and I opted for the rice.)

KEEP THINGS IN PERSPECTIVE

It was one of those long text-message conversations that really should have turned into a phone call. In a nutshell, one of my best friends may be coming to Key West for a wedding next year, and would I be willing to share any advice, tips or warnings for someone planning a wedding here?

Absolutely, I told her. Happy to do it.

I've attended an estimated 17 weddings over the past 13 years and hear frequent, often hilarious bridal anecdotes from my good friend Rob O'Neal, who has photographed more white dresses, clasped left hands, sunset backgrounds and "kiss the bride" moments than he cares to recall.

And then of course, there was my own wedding last April.

Fourteen months have now passed since our perfect day, and with time comes hindsight; teaching us today the lessons we needed to learn yesterday. Hindsight is a valuable tool – for anything you're going to do more than once. And despite all the statistics, no bride-to-be with a sparkling new ring on her left hand, ever refers to this as her first wedding. This is a one-shot deal and you want to get it right.

We did.

We planned it all ourselves, with my amazing parents and a fantastic caterer. I wouldn't have changed a thing – well, except for the two broken ribs Stan suffered two days before. (Try reminding 150 alcohol-fueled guests not to hug the groom or slap him on the back. Man, he was a trooper.)

As a 13-year local armed with the benefit of hindsight, and nothing to gain in commissions from my opinions, I offer these words to the hundreds of fiancées out there currently considering a Key West wedding:

There's a difference, an expensive difference, between an open bar and free booze. As soon as a wedding guest hears "open bar," that guest, who drinks nothing but Coors Light at home, will begin ordering shots of sambuca for himself and everyone in earshot. Narrow their options to beer, wine, rum and vodka with appropriate mixers. Anyone who can't find something they like among those choices shouldn't be at your wedding. Notice I didn't put tequila on the list. Trust me. Tequila never ends well; never.

Key West gets hot, really hot, from July to October. I'm not telling you to stay away in the summer, but there is no reason to make a man wear a jacket and tie for the duration of the ceremony and reception. And those floor-length bridesmaid dresses with the itchy crinoline lining were made for indoor, air-conditioned events. Consider short dresses and matching Hawaiian-type shirts. Otherwise your entire wedding party will hate you by the time you say, "I do." The same goes for the guests. They're on vacation. It's Key West, and they've spent a bunch of money to show up for your wedding. Don't piss them off by insisting they wear ties and pantyhose on a blazing afternoon.

Just say no to the Macarena, Electric Slide or Chicken Dance. Wedding guests only participate because they're expected to. (The free booze also plays a part, but believe me, no one walks into a wedding venue saying, "Man I hope we get to do the Macarena tonight.")

No one cares who designed your gown or how much it cost. If you can't be happy without a designer-label on the dress you'll wear exactly once, then I don't want to come to your wedding. And anyone who can't find their perfect dress among the thousands at David's Bridal is just an intolerable snob. Stunning dresses are available for less than $300 – believe me. Mine was less than $250, and I still gaze longingly at it in the back of the closet. On a related note, however, David's Bridal is not the place to get affordable bridal accessories. Yes,. It's more convenient to get everything from jewelry to bachelorette novelties in the same place, but don't expect any discount prices on these items. To be completely honest, my mom and I found my bridal earrings and necklace in Claire's Boutique on Duval Street for about $16. They were combined with an antique sapphire bracelet that had belonged to Stan's grandmother, and no one was the wiser – until now. I also picked up a little, white satin purse in the kids' section of Claire's for my wedding day necessities.

Something will go wrong. Know that. And deal with it. The only thing that can truly ruin a wedding is a miserable bride. Ask our photographer friend. It's what he calls "subject failure," and it has ruined hundreds of wedding photos.

Yes, it's your day, but that doesn't mean you can be a bitch. People have traveled a long way and are spending a lot of money to join you on this day. Don't give them any reason to regret it.

Have fun. This should be obvious, but we've all met brides who are so worried about a plastic figurine on top of an overpriced cake or the order of their bridesmaids from shortest to tallest that they make themselves miserable on what should be the happiest day of their life. This will be the only time you and your husband are surrounded by all the people you love most in the world, so enjoy it. I know I did.

Origins

This column was borne of my frustration with the wedding industry. I feel so badly for out-of-town brides who have to put their trust in someone else to plan their Key West wedding, not knowing what kind of "arrangements" all the vendors have with each other when it comes to commissions for recommending bands, venues, florists or caterers.

TRAVEL:
VACATIONS BEGIN
& END IN KEY WEST

PRICELESS

As you read this, I am out of the country, most likely with a drink in my hand and some type of food within reach.

I realize many of you read the newspaper at 8 a.m. on Sunday, and a cocktail may seem inappropriate to some (not all). But I am in Mexico right now on a four-day Carnival cruise with 11 of my best friends to celebrate my 30th birthday and the birthdays of Jen Johnson and David Sloan, who, by the way, are both older than me. This celebration will not be accomplished with Diet Coke and lemonade, and an international incident is imminent.

I do not have access to a cell phone or laptop and have no idea what is happening in Key West.

I do have access to a 24-hour pizza buffet, fine dining options, free room service, a casino, a pool (with a waterslide), a Lido Deck, cabin stewards and about seven bars. This is working out just fine.

The trip began (as many of our adventures do) over a few drinks on Sunday afternoon about six weeks ago. A friend had suggested we plan a trip in May for my 30th birthday. We were ambitious at the time and apparently overestimating our net worth as we tossed around ideas like Belize and Costa Rica with little or no research. Sure, those places are supposed to be cheap — once you pay for the flight and find a hotel that the girls and gay men will actually stay in.

David then suggested the cruise idea. Food and hotel are included in the trip and because it departed from Miami, did not require airfare. The dates were set, and a few phone calls were made to friends in Orlando who make any perfect vacation even better.

The numbers of people in attendance changed bit by bit, as people decided to screw their credit card bill, take a few days off and get on the boat. Unfortunately, there are two locals not currently aboard Carnival Imagination. So let me assure Gregg and Michelle that we miss them terribly (but not too terribly as to be having a bad time, because we know they wouldn't want that for us.)

I got in touch with a fantastic Carnival agent named Kari, who by now wishes she was also on the ship with us. She hooked us up with cabins near each other, reassured we first-time cruisers about what to bring and what to wear. (Of course, by now, one of us has probably been reprimanded for throwing some article of clothing over the railing, but we won't tell Kari.)

Rob O'Neal, who took the plunge about a week after hearing his friends yammer endlessly about a trip that was still 35 days away, announced to everyone's delight that he would indeed be joining us on the Lido Deck — and at the bacon section of the buffet — for four days.

I can promise you we have had to retrieve him from said buffet for a group activity on more than one occasion by now, and he'll have the photos to prove it. It is also likely that I have pushed aside some poor 12-year-old while in line for the waterslide and that more than one of us has fallen down, spilled a drink or gotten lost on the way to our own cabin.

Not to worry, this is all in a day's vacation for this group and we live by the motto: If you're gonna be dumb, you better be tough.

The way I figure it, this trip is like a credit card commercial:

Four-day Carnival cruise: $449
Bar tab for four-day Carnival cruise: $500
Bail money for Mexican jail: $1,000
Spending your 30th birthday on the Lido Deck with 11 of the best people you know: Priceless.

ROADTRIP

A simple mention of the word evokes adolescent images of late-night plans, misguided motives and generally irresponsible travel. Leaving at 2 a.m. to have a full first day at the destination always sounded like a good idea – until about 7 a.m. The oil change everyone's car needed lost its importance when New Orleans was a mere six states and 14 hours away.

Those trips made for some great memories, and I still have the photos taken by the side of the road at each state line.

Florida is a tough on road trips if you're interested in actually changing states. Our location at the very bottom makes it even tougher. In Jersey, if you drive four hours south, you'll visit three states. I drove through five of them and our nation's capital during my eight-hour journeys home from college in North Carolina.

But last weekend we spent 14 hours in a killer rental car and only made it to Tampa. I know, I know, Tampa is only eight hours away. You've apparently never traveled with me. I'm a bit of a treat. My water addiction has led to a rest stop addiction and my navigation leaves much to be desired. Much. A lot. Everything.

But I digress. The trip was to begin with a planned departure time of 7 a.m. I was packed the night before and the alarm was set. I hadn't screwed up a.m. and p.m. and the alarm actually went off. It blared loudly next to my right ear – for two hours with slight, eight-minute reprieves every time I smashed the snooze button.

When I finally realized what was happening, it was 8:08 a.m. We were on Stock Island and heading north in the rental car a little after 10 a.m. (three hours behind schedule for anyone keeping track.)

What could have been a silent and sulking ride north turned into a decision to take our time getting to Tampa, where we were meeting friends to go to Busch Gardens the next day.

Things then went rather smoothly with a pizza lunch in the Upper Keys – until we hit the turnpike and I sailed 27 miles past the exit for the Tamiami Trail, where we planned to stop at Loop Road and check on the alligators. (That's 54 miles and another additional hour to the trip for those still calculating.)

Upon realizing my huge mistake, a quick exit and U-turn were necessary. Apparently, I was trying to make up for all lost time with one U-turn that spilled the cooler, sent grapes, ice, granola bars and Diet Cokes all over the back seat, and slammed my reclining passenger into the side of the car just before he glanced up to see another car inches from his face.

Oh, the centripetal force also threw a suitcase into the compartment behind my seat that also held a pair of sunglasses (not mine, of course.) Those were, as you've probably guessed, scratched. At this point I was amazed I hadn't been dismissed from the car and sent home on foot.

Luckily the only thing left to do (following the clean-up of the backseat, the drying off of a birthday gift and the rearrangement of the cooler) was to burst out laughing, incredulous that so many things could go wrong and two people could still be on not only speaking, but laughing terms.

Things were looking up at this point, and we only had about nine hours left. A bumpy trek down Loop Road, always one of my favorite road trip diversions, showed alligators, rats, alligator gars, giant grasshoppers, huge buzzards and other birds whose names I should know (sorry, Mark Hedden, I'll work on it).

Despite serious traffic issues on I-75, and one buggy outdoor dining experience, all went well along the state's west coast and we arrived at our destination, road weary but still speaking and laughing around 11 p.m. The rest of the weekend was much less harrowing and so much fun. I didn't drive much.

The trip home was remarkably shorter, but no less enjoyable. And to think the next excursion involves air travel. What could possibly go wrong? Let's not pull at that string.

Happy trails.

A DIFFERENT WORLD

I experienced one of those tiny life epiphanies a few weeks ago; well, maybe not so tiny considering it may have saved my life.

I was reminded that when water skiing unsuccessfully, one can stop the entire lake from rushing up one's nose by doing just one thing: letting go of the rope.

It's a simple concept, really, but one that didn't come as naturally as it should have last week in the mountains of North Georgia while the ski boat continued to drag me around for several moments after I had face-flopped into the lake. To his credit, the driver of the boat, well aware of my failure, was already circling back, assuming, of course, that I was no longer attached to the vessel.

Once my sinuses had drained, I gave it another shot, and eventually rediscovered the thrill of water skiing. This was my first time doing it under the towering, green Southern Blue Ridge Mountains, and it was spectacular.

With the dust knocked off my skiing skills, I embarked on a week of it during a recent adventure that could not have been better timed.

As Tropical Storm Faye approached the Florida Keys, I was sipping moonshine (not a big fan, by the way) and listening to two friends play guitar on a boat in the middle of Lake Burton under stars we could almost touch.

I wasn't forced to write a single newspaper article about people filling their gas tanks, buying plywood and discussing their own storm predictions. It was a beautiful thing, especially when we knew our friends and the island were safe.

I was out of cell phone range most of the week, as I refused to sell a major organ to pay the outrageous "roaming charges." Instead I relished the freedom of water skiing all morning, lounging on a raft all afternoon and trout fishing in the evening. I even shot guns; big ones.

At one point we were actually wading up the river where they filmed "Deliverance," and laughing about the T-shirt in a marina gift shop that read, "Paddle faster, I hear banjo music."

While the others in our trio were expertly manipulating fishing rods and walking gracefully through mud and rocks in the river, I was several yards behind, thrashing through it, slipping regularly and reciting a steady mantra of, "No snakes, no snakes, no snakes."

The fishing rod became the sword with which I planned to slay any water moccasins that approached. Either that, or I would fling the rod at it, scream like a baby-sitter in a horror movie and drop dead of a heart attack. But at least I had a plan.

Fortunately, my mantra worked. Of course, it also scared off all trout in the immediate and not-so-immediate vicinity, but it's not like anyone was expecting ME to catch dinner.

Water moccasins, trout fishing and moonshine.

Oh yes, we were in the South.

Although I spent four college years in North Carolina, this here was a more "countrified world." I adapted readily and loved every minute of it.

With real biscuits and gravy, fried green tomatoes, fresh vegetables and the beautiful scenery, I was saying "y'all" in no time.

The hospitality of our hosts was unparalleled and we've already invited ourselves back for the autumn leaves. The lake may a bit chilly, but the cabin is warm and inviting and there's always the moonshine to scorch the back of the throat.

It was a vacation to remember and repeat, and one I had never before experienced.

Of course it took a while for this Jersey Shore girl to remember that the tide doesn't change in a lake, and the water isn't salty. But I had plenty of time for this realization while forgetting to let go of the ski rope.

IN THE AIR AND ON THE WATER

I had no idea I had fallen asleep on the plane until I experienced one of those embarrassing, startled wake-ups. You know the kind: your whole body tenses, you inhale sharply and audibly; then a foot kicks out uncontrollably so your shin nails the rod of the seat in front of you. Moments later, when you realize where you are, you notice sheepishly that the people around you are glancing over with a bemused smirk and raised eyebrow.

That was me Tuesday afternoon on my return flight from the Bahamas, where I had a glorious long weekend with my husband. As I may have mentioned, and as everyone is sick of hearing, Stan's fishing a marlin tournament over there for 11 weeks this spring and summer. I may also have mentioned ad nauseam that I hate it when he's away and miss my best friend terribly.

But on the bright side, this isn't "Deadliest Catch" or anything. He's not freezing his ballyhoo off in icy, 30-foot swells near the Arctic Circle or anything. It's the Bahamas, mon; home of pink sand, smiling islanders and the freshest conch around. Oh I know, there's still conch in our Florida Keys waters, and we all know some longtime cavaliers who still catch them clandestinely for their own nostalgic enjoyment, but if I can't afford to pay the power bill and the cable bill in the same month, then I certainly can't afford the fines associated with harvesting the alien-looking mollusks locally.

But I felt like a million bucks lounging on the bow and being rocked to sleep by a stunning 50-foot Hatteras all weekend. You see, the owners of the boat he's working on graciously buy me a plane ticket every four weeks. It's sort of an industry standard in that world, and one that I fully endorse.

And if the Bahamas excursion wasn't enough, I was also treated the weekend prior to a trip to Orlando, where my parents were meeting my brother, sister-in-law and nephews for a Disney extravaganza.

That weekend happened to be my birthday, and who can argue with a great Italian dinner in the world of Epcot, followed by one of the best fireworks displays I've ever seen? I'm having a hell of a birthday month, I must say. Of course, I still haven't paid the cable or power bill, but I'm working on those.

I did have to pay $3 for a bottle of water in the Orlando airport, but these things happen.

Unfortunately, the fun is not always in the journey, but really does happen in the destination, and there are few things in life that can turn us against our fellow human beings faster or more completely than air travel.

I know I've said this before, but it bears repeating: How can any American still be surprised and a little put off when asked to remove their shoes in the security line? I'm hoping that if they had been at all aware of this startling, new phenomenon in airports, perhaps they wouldn't have opted for boots that lace up their entire calf. Then again, I've given up on assuming people will make any logical decisions when they're near me in an airport.

For instance, there should be no reason for anyone to have to walk through the metal detector more than twice. I'll give everyone one freebie to allow for the forgotten change in one of the 19 pockets on guys' cargo shorts. But I'll never understand why a guy takes his belt off after the machine beeps the first time, but doesn't take the keys out of his pocket until the second or third time through, after he's also jettisoned the watch and then the sunglasses from his shirt pocket – all on individual attempts.

Also, how can some people, usually women I'll admit, look at their giant Louis Vuitton suitcase and honestly believe it will fit in the overhead compartment? We've all seen these huffy women; trying in vain to shove the thing into the space and then blaming a flight attendant when told it will have to be checked. And let's not forget the peril we've all faced when the chick, who's probably the one from security in the lace-up boots, finally gives up and lets the luggage swing down onto the heads of those already seated.

Finally, I have to wonder at the airline industry's ability to move a jumbo jet safely across the Atlantic Ocean when they can't come up with a PA system that can be heard clearly from the restaurant directly next door to the departure gate in a large, metropolitan airport. (Let me give credit here to Key West International Airport, where the announcements were clear, the security agents were friendly, and things went quite smoothly on the way to Orlando. Sadly, I couldn't fly commercially from here to the Bahamas and thus endured the nightmare that is Miami International Airport.)

But back to the static. When's the last time you were confident enough

134

in what you heard over the loudspeaker to remain seated and finish your cocktail at the airport lounge? No, we end up walking over to the gate anyway "just to make sure" they hadn't started boarding our flight.

We generally make this little, luggage-laden trek to the gate right after pausing mid-sentence to tilt our head and look at the ceiling. It's the universal sign for, "Hang on, I need to try and hear whether they're calling my flight."

Sadly, the amplified frustration doesn't always end once we're inside that flying capsule of closeness. The flight attendants come across loud and clear during their safety briefing, but the pilot, while only about three feet from the flight attendants, sounds like he's shouting his altitude report from outside on the wing.

Despite all the usual travel aggravations, flying undoubtedly brings people together. Planes often bring people too close together, but airports at least see as many happy reunions as tearful goodbyes, and who doesn't smile just a little at the sight of a kid running full tilt into his grandmother's hug or a husband holding flowers and eagerly searching for the face of his returning wife?

For the past two weekends, I was reunited with the people I cherish most in the world, and all the little nuisances are well worth the sight of those faces at my final destination. Plus, when the trip is over, and it's time to head home, Key West is never a bad place to end a vacation – with or without cable.

A TALE OF TWO ISLANDS

As I write this week's column, a pile of folded clothes awaits placement in my suitcase for a Saturday flight to Atlantic City.

Stan and I are heading to my hometown at the Jersey Shore, which has been forever insulted by the ridiculous MTV reality series of the same name.

We now have to convince anyone who asks that we're not going to spend our vacation in a mall surrounded by women with high hair and huge accents.

We're going to the barrier island town of Ocean City, with six miles of beach, two miles of boardwalk and an endless supply of real pizza and great cheesesteaks.

Key West and Ocean City are both islands and are both dependent on sun-seeking tourists.

But that's pretty much where the similarities end.

For example, Ocean City is not what you'd call "alluring" come January, when the shops are boarded up and the sky is bleak over a churning, gray ocean.

But it snaps back to life every spring as seasonal residents show up with the first load of groceries and clean sheets. They open their houses, take the porch furniture out of the garage and slap a coat of paint on the outside shower. Every Shore house has an outside shower, and there's usually a waiting list for it every afternoon around 4, when the sunburned masses schlep their way home from the beach at the end of the street.

The families with young kids lumber slowly toward the house. Broken sunglasses perch precariously on the nose of a stooped father, barely visible amid a gritty, wet mountain of sand toys, coolers, diaper bags and an umbrella that keeps trying to burst open on the sidewalk. Mothers are usually carrying a sleeping infant wrapped in a giant beach towel, or holding the hand of a worn-out youngster hovering between utter exhaustion and the inevitable second wind that inflates their tiny spirit at the mere mention of boardwalk rides, miniature golf or soft-serve ice cream.

Yep, in the springtime, while Key West is yawning its way into a humid lull, the Jersey Shore is buzzing with anticipation of yet another summer; one that's filled with beach chairs, paperbacks, boardwalk carousels and

136

front-porch reunions.

And unlike Key West, Ocean City laws do not allow us to carry around cocktails in plastic cups. I know, I know, open containers are technically illegal in Key West, but only if you're homeless.

Instead of the eye-popping, breast-baring Fantasy Fest parade, Ocean City offers the annual, family-friendly Baby Parade, and body paint is never an acceptable costume.

The Ocean City boardwalk, as the island's main tourism thoroughfare, would be comparable to Duval Street.

Of course, the Dirty Joke Guy would be replaced by a clown selling Mylar balloons in the shape of Spiderman, Barbie, or whichever movie character is popular that year.

The bars would all be pizza joints, fresh-squeezed lemonade shacks, miniature golf courses or salt water taffy shops.

Ocean City does have its share of T-shirt shops, although none of their owners have ever been caught charging Japanese tourists $487 for an iron-on decal.

I've never seen a drag queen in Ocean City, although the resemblance is striking between our southernmost "ladies," and the shore's most weathered and leathery women on the beach.

They're the ones permanently affixed to beach chairs in the exact same spot on the sand from morning till sunset. Most of them resume their position down here in Florida sometime around October, before their tan fades completely.

Yes, the differences between Ocean City and Key West are too numerous too count, yet they have one thing in common.

Me.

When in Key West, I tell my friends that I am going "home" for vacation every summer, but when I'm sitting happily on my parents' front porch discussing life at the end of the road, it's this crazy, hot island that I refer to as "home."

In recent years, I've stopped trying to figure out which one is accurate, because they both work.

If home really is where the heart is, then I have two – homes, that is, not hearts.

The first is where I grew up, learned to drive, got my first job and met my first boyfriend. It holds my parents, the house I know intimately and hundreds of nostalgic landmarks.

The second is the place that I chose. Or rather, it chose me.

It's where I continued growing up, formed the tightest friendships, and met my last boyfriend.

Both places have made me who I am, and both will always be home – with or without drag queens and Spiderman balloons.

Now if you'll excuse me, I have a suitcase to pack. I'm going home.

LIFE LESSONS

THE END OF ONE ERA; THE START OF ANOTHER

First comes love, then comes marriage. Then comes....

Yeah, right, let's not get that rumor started.

There's no baby carriage on our horizon yet. And that's a good thing, because as it stands, there's no room for a baby or its carriage in our apartment.

In fact, there's barely enough room for two adults who, in the past month, have amassed an impressive array of brand new belongings. We're finding space for new dishes, towels, sheets, kitchen appliances, vacuums, picture frames, tool sets, artwork, area rugs, mirrors, storage trunks and a 52-inch flat-screen, plasma television.

Our wedding guests were a most generous group, and we could not be happier – or more grateful.

But our place has gotten crowded, and so begins the quest for a new home.

I have loved my little Simonton Street abode since friends had to remove a piece of molding to get the couch in the door exactly 10 years ago.

Like many chopped-up, old Key West homes, the place comes with its share of idiosyncrasies.

The front door opens directly into the bedroom, and French doors in the bathroom lead to the porch.

For five years, the magnetic strip around the freezer door was the only thing keeping it attached. The hot water scalds within seconds and the unearthly whine and shudder of air in the pipes occasionally wakes the neighborhood.

In 10 years, there has been one rat, two scorpions, a few wasps, several geckos, swarms of termites and more than 40 couch surfers.

The house is 64 steps from Fausto's, 40 from Chinese food and just a block from Duval Street.

And the people around us have turned the block into a true neighborhood, where people pay attention, look out for one another, help in any way they can and always know what time we come home at night.

The owners and property managers have kept the rent truly affordable and I wouldn't trade my time here for all the world. If only we could simply add another room and stay forever.

This place has seen countless kitchen mishaps and two well-documented painting adventures. There have been thousands of late nights, afternoon naps and morning rushes.

This was the first place that was entirely mine. Any dirty dishes were in the sink because I had left them there. I could eat any food in the refrigerator, because I, not a roommate, had bought it.

There's plenty of room here for one person, and just enough for the two who have lived here for the past two years.

I happily made room for Stan's treasured fish mounts, handmade bows and arrows, humidor, family photos, fishing rods, tackle boxes and tools.

But it's now time to make new memories in a home we create together.

I want him to decide where the couch will go, and which wall will support the new television.

While I don't expect him to carry me over any new threshold, I do want the name "Miles" above the door.

It would help if that door opens into a large one-, or affordable two-bedroom place that fits the budget of a starving writer and a hard-working fisherman.

We don't need anything fancy, and we haven't even given notice for our Simonton Street home.

The search is just beginning, and we'll welcome all suggestions.

In the meantime, first comes love, then comes marriage, then comes….a yard sale.

It's the only way to clear a path through the living room.

ENLIGHTENED YARD-SELLING

Who steals from a yard sale?

I couldn't believe what I was seeing a few weeks ago on Washington Street, where an organized crime ring was operating in someone's front yard. While perusing a table of 25- cent books, I overheard a woman asking, in broken English, the price of a large bedspread. She was holding it open and sort of shaking it in front of the hostess, who had been courteous enough to provide coffee in Styrofoam cups for her early-morning customers.

While the potential buyer began intense negotiations for the bedspread, two of her shady cohorts smoothly slipped two blouses and a cheap little alarm clock into their oversized totes. I looked around with wide eyes, but didn't see any other witnesses, so I cleared my throat and said "Excuse me," to one of the women with a bulging purse. She ignored me until I repeated myself and asked loudly whether she had forgotten to pay for the shirt and clock. At that point she narrowed her eyes and muttered something in a different language while moving quickly toward the street. Her associates followed immediately, no longer interested in the bedspread.

I didn't know what to do, and the thieves were nearly to their car when I told the hostess that the women had stolen from her. That's when my frustration with the human race changed to embarrassment and pride.

The Washington Street woman frowned and looked over at the women hiking up their skirts and piling into a dilapidated Oldsmobile. While I was about to fish a pen out of my purse and write down the license plate number (I truly have no time or tolerance for thieves), the hostess shrugged and said, "I figured something was going on. I can only hope they need those things more than I needed their four dollars."

Her compassion and forgiveness stopped me in my tracks. Here was a woman who would likely have given the items to the thieves, but they didn't take the time to learn that. They didn't give her a chance to offer, and they had no idea whether their four dollars would have helped the woman keep her power on for another month.

More likely, she was just trying to get rid of some stuff, and whatever she didn't sell would end up at the Salvation Army. Still, one never knows. And you don't take things that don't belong to you. It's one of the first rules you learn, right up there with "Don't throw sand," and "Don't hit your sister."

Hell, as one of the Ten Commandments, it was one of the first rules ever. But this woman — I wish I had asked her name — was able to see things from a more enlightened perspective, and I thank her for opening my still sleepy eyes on that Saturday morning.

That said, as I eye my own superfluous belongings in preparation for a yard sale in the coming months, I must warn my potential customers that this sense of enlightenment likely will have faded by then. And if I catch you waving a towel at me while your friends pocket my picture frames, I'll pound you with a fondue pot.

On the other hand, if you ask nicely, I may just give you the damn towel.

A KEY WEST BABY STORY

There was only one candle on the strawberry birthday cake Friday night, but little Eva didn't care. In fact, she was more interested in sticking a straightened index finger into the whipped-cream icing than in blowing out her first birthday candle.

Actually, I'm not even sure a 1-year-old has mastered the skill of pursing the lips and blowing. But it didn't matter. She was having a big time, surrounded by people eager to celebrate her first year of life.

Friday was her very first birthday, quite a milestone, and she has probably grown, changed and learned more in the past year than she will in all the coming years between birthdays. It's been amazing to watch the transformation from bald little infant to animated little girl.

Last Sept. 17, I sat in a hospital room at Lower Keys Medical Center holding my best friend's brand-new daughter. To be quite honest, she didn't do much. But then, she didn't have to, and everyone was happy to sit and stare at the tiny snoozing infant who rarely cried and smiled early.

But that all changed quickly enough, and the little bundle of soft cloth and tiny toes turned into a real person with a daring personality and a huge smile. Michelle and I have often remarked that we can't remember what we used to talk about before there was a baby to occupy our attention and make us laugh.

She quickly learned to sit up, roll over and reach for things — Eva, not Michelle. She is convinced the sounds she makes are actual words, even if no one else can yet interpret them. She speaks her own language of gibberish, inflections and raised eyebrows that will eventually become sentences and questions. She started walking at 9 1/2 months, and discovered the joys of wooden spoons banged against pots and pans. She got her first pair of tiny, pink Nikes and drinks from her very own sippy cup. She has little sapphires in her newly pierced ears, and didn't even cry when the lady pierced them.

She has gone from a sleeping blob who couldn't focus her eyes on anything more than 8 inches away, to a real little kid— walking, talking and understanding so much of this world that was foreign to her just 12 months ago. She watches TV and pushes the buttons on any cell phone she can find. She eats real food now and knows the meaning of a firm, "No," when she wanders near the television cords.

And she cracks herself up when she ventures there again with a devilish gleam in her eye and a smile she knows will disarm anyone's anger. She no longer fits in the small, pink fleece-lined basket that was her bed for the first few months, and her first Christmas dress looks miniature now compared to her blue jeans and sundresses.

She's been swimming in our pool and puts her head fearlessly under water. She dances in Uncle Stan's arms while he makes up funny songs, and she knows which low cabinet holds our wooden spoons and pots.

It's been a huge first year for the little one I call Ladybug, and for her parents, who slipped seamlessly and impressively into parenthood.

There was much cause for jubilation Friday night on Hilton Haven, and while Eva carried around the bottle of milk she still drinks before bed, the grown-ups enjoyed more adult beverages to help with the celebration.

She'll have other birthdays — lots of them. Some will mark momentous years, symbolizing kindergarten, double digits, teenage angst, a driver's license, official adulthood and the right to buy beer. Others will stand simply for another year of life, another year of learning. But this first birthday, ending the first year, although it's one that Eva will never remember, was an event her parents will never forget, and one I was proud to be a part of.

Happy Birthday, Ladybug. Aunt Mandy and Uncle Stan love you.

THIS ISN'T ALL THERE IS

Listen up, kids. Stop texting for a minute. Read something other than a tiny phone screen and don't roll your eyes at me. This is important, because, by now, some adult has told you at least once that these are the best days of your life, and that you need to savor this time of adolescence.

I'm here to tell you they're wrong. These are not the best days of your life – at least, they don't have to be.

When adults tell kids these are the best days of their life, we're telling them that middle school and high school are as good as it gets. And for most of us, thankfully, it's just not true.

I wouldn't want it to be true for my own kids. I don't want them to peak in high school and then live the remaining 80 percent of their life in decline, pathetically and constantly rehashing their "glory days."

Thankfully, that's a lifetime sentence reserved for the bullies who made school, and life, miserable for others.

The kids who relish in the high school cliques and in the constant harassment of smaller, smarter students better be enjoying themselves now, because, for them, it's all there is.

Amid the meathead bullies' mean-spirited jeers and smirks are the kids who are miserable every single morning. They dread the tortuous bus ride and school hallways filled with Neanderthals, who are always the sons and daughters of bullies.

But there is a light at the end of the tunnel for the kids who haven't hit their growth spurt; whose acne hasn't yet cleared and whose mind is more agile and athletic than their body. I just want to reassure you that things do get better. There is life after high school; so much life. And the universe, in its infinite karmic wisdom, tends to get even with the people who make life miserable for others.

Trust me, decades later, the same sneering morons will be reliving the same championship game and laughing about the same stupid pranks with their same band of cronies. Hell, they'll probably still be bullying people as adults in the workplace.

Kids, take a look at today's schoolyard bullies. Then take a look at their parents. Bullies breed bullies. They accomplish their goals through fear and intimidation, because they don't have enough class or intelligence to do it any other way.

Of course you should enjoy childhood as much as possible, but I know you'll never appreciate its joys and freedoms until it's all over. Kids haven't experienced anything but childhood, so there's no basis for comparison.

I get that. And yes, adulthood presents its own share of challenges. I'm not going to lie to you. Seemingly overnight, the government starts taking 20 percent of your paychecks. The refrigerator is only full when someone pays for groceries and the air-conditioning only keeps us cool when the power bill gets paid.

Despite all this, I wouldn't trade adulthood for all the prom dates in the world.

There are no tests or report cards. There is no 7 a.m. bus ride and you can decide all by yourself whether you're sick enough to stay home for the day.

Childhood can and should be a magical time for everyone, but let's stop telling our kids that life doesn't get any better than high school football games, homecoming dances and cafeteria food.

It gets way better – well, at least for most of us.

For you bullies, you evolutionary U-turns, well, you deserve as much happiness as you've brought to others. And I hope you're enjoying your youth, because your future looks bleak.

FLYING FREE OVER THE KEYS

I didn't throw up and I didn't wet my pants.

Normally, keeping my breakfast inside my body and maintaining bladder control are not front-page accomplishments I announce to thousands of people on a Thursday morning.

Then again, I'd never spent a Wednesday afternoon in the cockpit of an F/A-18 Hornet. But there I sat grinning stupidly and reminding myself to breathe as U.S. Navy Crew Chief Chris Fancher secured the 11 buckles that would hold me in place for the next 45 heart-stopping minutes.

"Don't scream," he said with a smirk as he handed me a blue helmet and reminded me not to touch anything in the cockpit —especially not the loop of the ejection handle that rested innocently between my legs, but would immediately launch me and the pilot, U.S. Marine Maj. Len Anderson, onto a "bonus ride" that really wasn't necessary.

Fancher had spent an hour with Todd Swofford, Gary Freeland and me — the three media representatives selected to experience the most exciting ride of our lives. The ride came three days before the Blue Angels are set to demonstrate their skill, precision, strength and courage at the weekend air show.

Fancher allowed plenty of time for questions and went over the physiology of flying at the speed of sound and "pulling Gs" that would press us into our seats as the blood left our heads and tried to puddle around in our feet — along with any other puddles that might already exist down there.

He went over the effective, yet entirely unattractive "hook" maneuver in which you try to flex all the muscles in your body to force the blood (and consciousness) back into your brain. (Thanks, Chris, because the maneuver worked and my vision only got blurry once. Note: It's not a look you want to demonstrate on a first date.)

The anticipation mounted as Fancher handed out blue flight suits and led us out to the tarmac, where staff from the air station exchanged knowing, cryptic looks they apparently learn in flight school.

By the time I lowered myself into the cockpit, my face already hurt from smiling and my eyes didn't seem to be blinking at regular intervals. Fancher didn't seem alarmed as he reviewed the hook maneuver and showed me the controls I was not to touch.

149

He gave me the thumbs-up and climbed down as Anderson ascended the ladder and shook my hand before taking his seat in front of me. I'm not sure what he said, but I think I managed to blurt out my own name before he started laughing, sat down and tugged on his gold helmet, constantly reassuring me and explaining everything he was going to do, and everything I was going to feel.

But no one can prepare you for the immense rush of adrenaline that comes as the F/A-18 gathers speed instantly, hovers above the runway for a second and then launches straight up into the airspace surrounding the Naval Air Station Key West.

Anderson, through his laughter and my screams of glee, expertly maneuvered the plane through fluffy white clouds and tipped us on our side "to give me a better view" of the water below. We flew at the speed of sound. We flew upside-down. We flew on our side. We were weightless. We barrel rolled, diamond rolled, performed a split S and pulled a total of 7.4 Gs. (Again, not an attractive look for me.)

We also discussed the precision of the Blue Angels flight team, which flies with only 18 inches of space between their wings, and times everything perfectly according to "the Boss," who flies the lead plane and calls out the maneuvers over the radio. Of course, it must be a little easier to maneuver in formation without a crazed woman in the back who can't stop yelling, "This is awesome" broadcast deafeningly from my microphone to his helmet.

The trip could have lasted all day, and I would trade jobs with Anderson in a heartbeat (although he didn't seem real willing to give up his supersonic view of the world.)

I was exhausted. I was exhilarated. I was jealous of the pilots who get to experience that rush every day. And I was honored to be allowed into the cockpit of the F/A-18 Hornet as it went hurtling through the sky.

So when you're at the air show this weekend watching these guys deftly maneuver the multimillion-dollar insects through the skies, give them the thumbs-up, wish them well — and don't touch anything.

Godspeed, guys and thanks for the permanent smile!

'MUST-HAVE' EXPERIENCES

I've long believed there should be a requirement that anyone who eats in restaurants must first have worked in one.

The restaurant industry – and the world, for that matter – would be a better place if everyone perusing a menu knew what it means and how it feels to be "triple sat" while "in the weeds" just after the kitchen "86's" the most popular dinner special.

Do the terms bring back the familiar camaraderie of a summer restaurant job? Or do they remind you of last night's dinner crowd on Duval Street?

Either way, the restaurant experience is a valuable one that stays with you forever, and any former or current server, when dining, will always tip at least 20 percent, notice how many tables are in their waitress's station, whether the hostess is helping with drink orders and how many Saltines the family at the next table allows their toddler to pulverize and then throw on the floor.

Restaurant work should be one of life's prerequisites.

Have people like Kim Kardashian ever been forced to apologize to an unreasonable and irate customer who sends his soup and steak back three times? Has she ever noisily dropped a tray of entrees in the middle of a dinner rush, sending the kitchen staff into angry seizures? I think not, but would love to see it, and the experience may open her heavily made-up eyes to the difference between the real world and her so-called "reality" life.

Aside from restaurant work, there are several other lifetime achievements that may not qualify for any fancy awards, but would go a long way toward making the world a more equal and understanding place.

Here's what I'm thinking: Everyone should…

…live with a roommate who is not a relative or spouse.

…experience stitches, a cast or minor surgery that requires them to spend at least a few hours in a hospital.

…speak in public – as an adult in front of adults.

…deal with a flat tire. (I'm not requiring them to change it by themselves, but everyone should have to address the issue in some way, whether by calling AAA, the police or accepting help from a stranger.)

…dump and be dumped by a love interest.

…have to run for a flight, if only to appreciate the sense of relief that comes from arriving with sufficient time to grab a drink and wait at the gate for a few minutes.

...be forced to move or change schools sometime before high school. Yes, it's terrifying, but it really does build character while making all kids a little more sympathetic toward "the new kid."

...experience the anxiety of a job interview. (That's another thing I'm pretty sure the Kardashians and Paris Hiltons of the world have never had to do. And it shows.)

... know the name of the country's president and vice president, and watch at least one State of the Union address per year.

...be forced to change a diaper before having children,

...assemble a piece of furniture that shows up in a heavy, flat box,

...paint a room in their house,

...fail a test,

...cry at a movie. It could be anything from "Steel Magnolias" to "Band of Brothers," as long as there's a lump in your throat and a tear in your eye.

...have to kill a cockroach big enough to make that sickening crunch,

...attend a rock concert,

...experience at least one hangover. (Disclaimer to cover my butt: The drinking age in this country is 21, and alcohol can impair your judgment and make you do stupid, dangerous things.)

... visit a homeless shelter or other facility for people in need.

... embarrass themselves in public, whether by falling down, splitting their pants, dropping something or otherwise drawing unwanted attention from several onlookers..

These are just a few of my own thoughts. Feel free to add your own to the list of requirements for a "Real Life Achievement Award." Together, we can all make the world a more equal and understanding place the next time your entrée arrives before your soup.

You'll notice Kim Kardashian appears in multiple columns, but never in a flattering reference.

I dislike the woman on a cellular level and firmly believe she and the celebrity gossip reality machine represent everything that's wrong with America. In her world, shoes and handbags cost more than most people's first car, education is unnecessary and hard work is for people who don't have a reality show.

WHAT'S HOT, WHAT'S NOT

I made a socially responsible decision the other night in the checkout line at Albertsons; two if you count the reusable bags I brought with me. But I also refused to be sucked into Jennifer Aniston's adoption, Lindsay Lohan's shoplifting or a "Teen Mom's" mess.

I did not buy any of the celebrity gossip magazines that beckoned from their impulse-buy position just above the candy. I instead gave into the urge for a Take 5 bar. (Have you tried these things? Pretzel, peanut butter and caramel inside chocolate — pure genius.) But back to my social responsibility project, which must begin with my admission of guilt over the prior purchase of these gossip magazines.

I admit I followed the Angelina and Jennifer drama as it unfolded six or so years ago, and in doing so I also learned, on subsequent pages, of the Brittany Spears downward spiral and the divorce of those two reality buffoons, Jon and Kate, who had eight kids and no talent.

Those magazines became an occasional indulgence for an afternoon at the pool or as a break from my book during a three-hour flight. I'd be lured into some inane drama about Jessica Simpson's weight or a Kardashian's boyfriend. But no more. I decided the other night that I will no longer be a part of the embarrassment our country should be feeling at the attention we give these people.

Their dramas can unfold without me, because the attention and idolatry that we show celebrities and their tiny dogs is shameful, and the excess of Hollywood is surely one of the reasons other countries sneer at America.

We know what the Kardashians are doing every minute of the day, but in a survey, fully half of Americans between the ages of 18 and 24 could not identify the states of New York or Ohio on a map. The other half think the war in Iraq is being fought against Osama bin Laden in retaliation for the 9/11 attacks. I'm not making this up. An appalling 2006 CNN survey also showed that less than six months after Hurricane Katrina devastated New Orleans, 33 percent of young Americans couldn't point to the Big Easy on a map. We have much to be proud of in this country, but our priorities have gotten so far out of whack, it's terrifying.

More people vote for "American Idol" than for the president of the United States. We won't teach kids about birth control in school, but we'll make celebrities out of "Teen Moms," who get to be on MTV's hit show, and we'll keep building nurseries in high schools for the students' offspring. Paris Hilton, who didn't graduate from high school, but eventually "earned" her GED, has become a role model for young girls. For what? Going to parties, driving drunk, possessing cocaine, making sex tapes and saying, "That's hot"?

What's hot, Paris? What the hell are you talking about? It frustrates me to know that kids today are embarrassed to raise their hand and answer a question in class because it's not cool to be educated and involved.

On Thursday, a high school kid crossing Flagler Avenue gave me the finger and called me the most insulting word a woman can hear, while glaring at me in an obvious attempt to scare me. He was probably 15 years old, and, by the way, nowhere near the high school campus at 11 a.m.

He had stepped brazenly in front of my car, daring me not to stop, and then slowed down and strolled deliberately and casually past my front bumper, still glaring, but now with an added smirk because he was holding me up. Then came the name-calling and finger-raising — on his part; not mine, despite an overwhelming urge to run the kid over and then discuss the high points of social etiquette.

Who are these kids? I know, it's not all kids, and I've met some great ones in this town who will surely change the world someday; I know they will. But to the ones with that infamous chip on their shoulder: Pull your pants up and stop texting, you loser punks. How about having a real conversation with an adult, rather than rolling your eyes and turning back to your phone?

And what's with the constant anger? Is your life really so terrible that you have to go out of your way to make others dislike and fear you? Come on, you guys, get your act together and have some respect for yourself, and the world around you.

And while you're so busy loitering in front of a convenience store, pick up a map and find New York and Ohio, because knowledge, and an education — that's hot.

ABOUT THE AUTHOR

Mandy Miles was known as Mandy Bolen when she arrived in Key West, Fla. in July 1998.

Fresh out of college and drawn to the island of endless summer that had beckoned since her first visit at the age of 16, Mandy eagerly accepted a job as a fledgling reporter with the Key West Citizen.

She covered meetings of the county commission, city commission, school board and every other board that meets twice a month in the Florida Keys. She covered crimes, fires and first days of kindergarten. Then in 2001, she volunteered to try her hand at column-writing and started revealing her "Tan Lines" week by week.

People seemed to like what she wrote, so she kept doing it, often driving her friends crazy with the weekly panic of finding a topic. Eleven years later, she is still a fixture at the Key West Citizen, currently as its business editor and resident columnist.

Mandy Bolen became Mandy Miles on April 10, 2010, when she married the love of her life, Capt. Stan Miles, at the Key West Garden Club.

Cold drinks and colorful people in a hot town have provided enough education, insight and insanity to keep her notebooks full for more than a decade. But weekends in Key West still find Mandy lying on a pool float or beach chair – working on her "Tan Lines."